Homeschooling with a Meek and Quiet Spirit

by Teri Maxwell

CCI Communication Concepts, Inc.

Homeschooling with a Meek and Quiet Spirit

Ordering information:
Managers of Their Homes
2416 South 15th Street
Leavenworth, Kansas 66048
Phone: (913) 772-0392
Web: www.Titus2.com

Published by:
Communication Concepts, Inc.
www.we-communicate.com

ACKNOWLEDGEMENTS

Scripture taken from the HOLY BIBLE, KING JAMES VERSION.

ISBN 978-0-9669107-1-1

Printed in the United States of America

1 2 3 4 5 6 7 8 9

This book was created in Microsoft Word. QuarkXPress 4.0 and Adobe Photoshop 5.5 were used for layout and design. All computers were Windows based systems running Windows NT/2000.

Design by Christopher Maxwell.

This book is dedicated to:

My family–for without them I wouldn't have realized my need for a meek and quiet spirit.

My husband–who has supported and encouraged me.

The Lord Jesus Christ–Who continues daily to teach and instruct me in the way I should go.

Contents

Acknowledgments

I am most grateful for those in my life who encouraged and helped in making *Homeschooling with a Meek and Quiet Spirit* a reality. Writing a book is an impossible task for a homeschooling mother of eight children without the assistance and support of her family and others.

My husband, Steven, is the one who said the workshop "Homeschooling with a Meek and Quiet Spirit" needed to be written as a book. He figured out a way to give me several hours each day to write. Many, many times he read over the manuscript, offering suggestions and revisions. Steve set deadlines for completing the work and made decisions on whom to ask to do editing and proofreading. He is my greatest support and encouragement!

Before beginning the editing and proofreading process, we asked a friend, Holly, if she would be willing to read the manuscript and give her feedback on it. She did this for us in the two days before her family left on a Thanksgiving trip!

With only a few days' notice and a tight deadline, my sister, Tami, began to invest her heart and time in *Homeschooling with a Meek and Quiet Spirit.* Not only does she do a wonderful job with the editing, but she also writes me little encouraging notes as she goes along!

Rex Frazer, my father, worked tirelessly on editing and proofreading the manuscript. He willingly dropped the activities that normally fill his day to allow him to push our project through.

Our oldest daughter, Sarah, pitched in for three weeks going many extra miles to free more of my time for writing. She also gave up much of her personal time in order to read the manuscript and proof it.

Christopher, our second oldest son, is the one who takes the words we give him and makes it into a real book! He, too, put countless hours into this project.

What gratitude and joy fills my heart for each of these whom the Lord has put into my life at this time and for this purpose. I can see His hand working through them. May our praise be of Him!

Teri

Preface

I think homeschooling moms are a wonderful group of women! I am most pleased to be numbered among you. There isn't a more determined, dedicated set of women in the entire world! You have chosen an unpopular, difficult path that comes with little outside encouragement. Yet, you have set your face on obedience to the Lord and what you know is best for your children—no matter what it costs you personally!

Even so, there are issues homeschooling brings up that I find are very common to most of us who homeschool. These common issues speak of what happens inside our hearts when we become fully responsible for our children's education, when they are home with us all day every day, and when we add several hours' worth of homeschooling into a full schedule as a wife, mother, homemaker, and Christian.

Sadly, if we don't meet the challenges of homeschooling with a meek and quiet spirit, we find ourselves discouraged. This is the very last thing you or I need to have to deal with! We can cope with the myriad of daily difficulties and decisions that a homeschooling lifestyle brings with it, as long as we are having the right responses to them. Let us be fearful, worried, anxious, frustrated, irritated, or angry, and we know we are undermining all we want to accomplish by homeschooling. We do not like this!

Because I have walked the homeschooling path for many years, I know first-hand the struggle for a meek and quiet spirit. The memories from my early homeschooling years of often being worried and angry rather than having a meek and quiet spirit are unpleasant for me. My prayer is that as I share the work the Lord has done in my heart, mostly through homeschooling, you would be encouraged that He can do the same for you. I also desire that you could learn from the lessons He has taught me so that you would begin to have a meek and quiet spirit long before I did.

As I have presented the "Homeschooling with a Meek and Quiet Spirit" material in workshops, moms confide in me later, "Wow, I was surprised to see so many other moms here. I thought I would be the only one!" If you don't have the meek and quiet spirit you would like, I can assure you that you are not alone.

The journey to a meek and quiet spirit is a life-long one. I am still on it. I can look at where I was–angry and yelling–to where I am–occasionally frustrated with irritated tones in my voice–to where I want to be–the fruit of the Spirit always evident. I don't want you to think I have totally arrived at a meek and quiet spirit. I haven't! I also don't want you to believe this book will change you overnight. It will not; only Jesus Christ works in hearts! I do want to offer you hope that the path to a meek and quiet spirit is a worthy one to travel.

You will not find information in this book such as: the perfect handwriting curriculum, how to get your baby to sleep through the night, what consequence to use for a dawdling child, or which homeschool method is best for your family. Instead, you will discover the heart issues that will gently lead you to a meek and quiet spirit as you find solutions to each of those other specific areas. After all, no one has the answers to those questions except Jesus Christ.

Come along and join me as we seek the Lord to home-school with a meek and quiet spirit!

Homeschooling with a Meek and Quiet Spirit Study Guide is available for those who want to make the most of the book. You may order it from www.Titus2.com or 913.772.0392.

Chapter One

A Meek and Quiet Spirit

Thinking back on September of 1985 still evokes memories of the start of our homeschooling adventure. What an excited mommy I was that first day of homeschooling! With my third and first grader, plus a preschooler, I was delightedly expectant of this new role in my life. My attitude demonstrated quite a change of heart. Just a few years earlier, I had been the kind of mother who could hardly wait until her three children were all old enough to be in school. However, when Jesus Christ calls one to a task, He can also give the enthusiasm to go with it. I had that enthusiasm and more!

I remember sitting down with my third grader for his first homeschool "read out loud" session. One reason we had decided to homeschool was that this son was having trouble with reading. The pace at school moved too fast, and he was being left behind with a very negative, reluctant attitude toward reading.

I was looking forward to the opportunity to help my son develop a love for reading. We were simply going to slow down to a pace he could reasonably manage. We would read out loud together, snuggled up on the couch side by side, and I would be right there to help him over the rough spots—no pressure!

That day, as he began to read, it didn't take long until he was stuck on a simple word. "Sound it out," I said. Nothing came from him. "Come on, Nathan. What did your teacher tell you about how these letters sound?" He attempted the word, but the vowel sound wasn't right. "Try again, Son." He did—the same way he had before! Finally, in exasperation, I said the word for him, and we continued.

By the end of those first fifteen minutes of my dream homeschooling life, I had become a very frustrated mother. I was close to tears. Rather than being patient and loving, I had been short and irritable. I expected my seven-year-old son to sound out the very words he had struggled with at school! I felt I had failed. I wondered whether I was wise to take on this job of homeschooling. Maybe I just wasn't cut out for it.

The next day I awoke with renewed enthusiasm. I knew it would be better, because I would be mentally prepared for the struggles our reading session would present. Sadly, even with that knowledge, I continued to lose patience with my son when we read together.

Help, Lord!

It wasn't long before I was on my knees crying out to the Lord over the sin in my life during these daily fifteen minutes of reading. If homeschooling was to provide sweet, precious moments with my son, and if he was to make progress in learning to read, I needed a change of spirit! Not only that, but I deeply desired a meek and quiet spirit to replace the irritable, impatient, sometimes even angry one I was displaying.

The Lord showed me that my reactions during the reading sessions were sin. 1 Corinthians 13:4 tells me, "Charity suffereth long, and is kind." My love (charity) was not long suffering or kind. I needed to confess my sin to my Lord Jesus Christ (1 John 1:9). I also had to ask my son's forgiveness. As I prayed about our reading time, the Lord prodded me to develop a plan for those sessions. It went like this. When Nathan came to a word he didn't know, I encouraged him to sound it out. If he didn't have any idea where to start, I would very slowly begin sounding it out for him. Then, he was to sound out the word after me.

The Lord also showed me that I needed to praise Nathan abundantly for every little word he read correctly. I am not a "gushy" kind of person, so this felt very artificial to me. However, that little boy beamed as he worked through his readers, while his mom lavished on him, "Good boy, Nathan. That's it. Wonderful. Keep it up!"

What a difference a simple change in my spirit generated. No longer was I pushing for my agenda, feeling frustrated when progress wasn't realized according to my expectations. Rather, I had found I needed to see my wrong behavior as sin, deal with it biblically, and seek the Lord for solutions to the difficulties. I felt new joy, sitting by Nathan as he did his reading, once the Lord brought me from having a frustrated spirit to having a meek and quiet spirit.

Can you guess what happened once my spirit changed? Within a few short weeks, Nathan's reading had improved immensely. Soon he became a fluent reader and came to thoroughly enjoy reading, even doing it during his free time.

Our Goal

What about you? Did you begin your homeschooling adventure with a particular picture in your mind? It might have involved sweet, cooperative children who were eager to learn. They were going to be taught, cuddled, and loved by a smiling, patient, long-suffering mother. Sometime, perhaps as early as the first day of homeschooling, this idyllic vision was shattered by an irritated tone in Mom's voice. It could have been caused by trying to teach over the noise of a rowdy toddler or simply by a student dawdling over his schoolwork. No matter what it was that caused you to react, there was disappointment in your spirit that the reality of homeschooling didn't match the ideal.

I am convinced that a heart-felt goal homeschooling moms have for themselves is that they would teach their children with a meek and quiet spirit. 1 Peter 3:4 says, "But let it be the hidden man of the heart, in that which is not corruptible, even the ornament of a meek and quiet spirit, which is in the sight of God of great price." This verse, in context, is speaking of a meek and quiet spirit in a husband and wife relationship. However, it would certainly transfer well to describing the godly spirit of a homeschooling mother.

How is a meek and quiet spirit characterized? What comes to your mind when you hear these words? Let's spend some time with them so that we are thinking along the same line.

Meek

Webster's 1858 Dictionary definition of "meek" is "mild of temper, soft, gentle, not easily provoked or irritated." This is truly what we homeschooling moms desire so much! We know our children will be difficult at times (some days continually), but we want to be "not easily provoked or irritated." We long to be soft and gentle even while training, correcting, or disciplining our children.

Let me share a story from my life several years ago. On this day, meekness did not characterize me. I had three school-aged children plus a preschooler, a toddler, and a baby. I walked into the bathroom, in the middle of a busy school morning, to discover the toilet paper had been unrolled all over the floor. Do you know what I did? I sat down on the floor and cried! In frustration, I raised my heart to the Lord, "Lord, there are just too many of them and too few of me!" Of course, unrolled toilet paper was not the only thing that had happened in our home that morning, but it was the straw that broke the camel's back. Sometimes, as I consider that day, I wonder why it was so terribly monumental. However, it was big enough to me then that I can remember it vividly enough to tell you about it today.

I wish this had been my reaction instead: "Lord, those little guys are at it again. Thank you for giving them to me to love, teach, and train. Please, Lord, give me the energy I need to deal sweetly with them. Also, grant me the courage and wisdom to discipline them. I love them so much, Lord!" It would have characterized a meek and quiet spirit despite discouraging circumstances.

Quiet

"Quiet," according to Webster, means "peaceable, not turbulent, not giving offense, mild, meek, and contented." Here we have a word picture of our heart's desire for our own spirit. When everything appears to be falling in around us, we would like to be peaceable through it, just as Jesus was in the midst of the storm. When our children aren't making the academic or character progress hoped for, we want to be content, waiting for them to catch on. We would like to "live out" for our children the reality of resting in the Lord.

One of my children is much slower in his learning than the others have been. This son is my dawdler as well. When he sits down to do schoolwork, he is immediately up to sharpen his pencil, pat the dog on the way, wash his hands for good measure, check out what his sister is doing at the piano, and finally hop back to his work. My ingrained reaction is frustration and irritation. This one child takes much more of my time and energy than the others. I am discouraged because of the slow progress we make in areas he is struggling with. Can you see my wrong thinking and focus? Unfortunately, my eyes are on myself. My spirit is not quiet. If it were, I would be content with the way God made this child, and there would be no turbulence inside me.

Now contrast the days I lift my heart to the Lord in prayer for this son in the midst of his meandering or his struggle with a math lesson. I know the Lord cares infinitely more how this son of mine turns out than I ever could. The Lord is the One Who works in the minds and hearts of my children. He has called me to homeschool my son, so I can rest with a quiet heart when my eyes are on the Lord Jesus.

Biblical Examples

There are two people in the Bible whom Scripture recommends to us as examples of a meek spirit. In Matthew 11:29 Jesus says, "Take my yoke upon you, and learn of me; for I am meek and lowly in heart; and ye shall find rest unto your souls." Jesus described Himself as meek. Therefore, we can do no better than to pray for, and work toward, a meek spirit ourselves.

Why did Jesus have a meek spirit? I believe it was because He was in full submission to the Father. He did nothing of His own but only what the Father told Him to do. "Then said Jesus unto them, When ye have lifted up the Son of man, then shall ye know that I am he, and that I do nothing of myself; but as my Father hath taught me, I speak these things. And he that sent me is with me: the Father hath not left me alone; for I do always those things that please him" (John 8:28-29).

Jesus died to His will and fully surrendered to the will of the Father. If Jesus, God's Son, would surrender to the will of the Father, then that is my example to follow.

The second biblical person shouldn't surprise you. It is Moses. "Now the man Moses was very meek, above all the men which were upon the face of the earth" (Numbers 12:3). Moses was called to lead the children of Israel out of Egypt. One of his qualifications was meekness! As homeschooling moms, aren't we leading our children? Surely, we are wise to look at Moses' characteristic of a meek spirit and desire it for ourselves.

Moses was a leader. He had to make wise decisions. He had to motivate his followers to be obedient. He could do all of this because he was meek. What made him meek? I would suggest that, as with Jesus, it was his intimate, personal time with the God Who had called him to lead the children of Israel.

My Own Meek and Quiet Spirit Journey

Teaching with a meek and quiet spirit is dear to me because I hear the discouragement many moms share from their homeschooling journey. These moms are seeking a meek and quiet spirit. Let me share a couple of their notes with you.

"I feel like a failure as a homeschooling mom! My six-year-old daughter and I were studying yesterday. She was to write the number that comes after 10. She said she didn't know. When I told her to count from 'one,' she did and said, 'eleven.' When I told her to write that number, she said she didn't know how! We have already done kindergarten and are now doing 1st grade. I have to admit that my enthusiasm for homeschooling does not meet my husband's desire. I guess it must be showing up in my teaching." Linda

"I'm an only child. I know nothing about siblings, but my oldest two children are driving me nuts. It is a constant 'I'm first,' 'Do my hair first.' There is continual whining from my four-year-old. The six-year-old acts as if he's in charge with his brother. The six-year-old is unhappy if the four-year-old (who is bright) watches us do schoolwork. All are fussing at the baby (one year old) who is into their toys—which they left unattended. HELP!!!!" Carol

"I don't know what is wrong with me lately. This is my second year homeschooling an eight-year-old daughter and a five-year-old son. Everything was going great until recently. I don't know what has happened. My daughter is developing an attitude so she and I clash almost daily. I have NO motivation to homeschool, clean the house, or get

on any kind of schedule. I know that homeschooling is God's Will for our lives but recently I just don't know if I can handle it anymore. I have really been considering checking into a Christian school and going back to work. Does anybody else ever struggle with these problems?"
Samantha

I have struggled with battles similar to the stories you just read. I could have written those words! When my children were much younger, I would respond angrily to these kinds of situations. I hated my reaction, but at times felt powerless against it. The Lord showed me that I was, indeed, powerless, but He wasn't. "Being confident of this very thing, that he which hath begun a good work in you will perform it until the day of Jesus Christ" (Philippians 1:6).

Through the past ten years, the Lord has begun to teach me wonderful lessons about how to have a meek and quiet spirit. I am still on that journey toward a meek and quiet spirit, but I want to encourage those of you who are discouraged with yourself that the Lord can change us. I am so grateful to not be the yelling mom I was at one time. I still want to learn not to have an irritated tone in my voice–ever–with my children. However, I know that just as the Lord has brought me from where I was, He will continue to move me forward as I press toward the goal of the high calling in Christ Jesus (Philippians 3:14). He will do the same for you, no matter where you are in the process of a meek and quiet spirit!

Meek and Quiet Spirit Robbers

Think with me for a moment about your homeschool day. What robs you of your meek and quiet spirit?

Did the alarm clock scream at you when it seemed you had just closed your eyes?

Is the baby hungrily wailing in the middle of your scheduled time with the Lord?

Are the children bickering first thing in the morning?

Is there an unmade child's bed you notice that was supposed to have been made an hour earlier?

Do you have stacks of laundry that continue to grow? Is the kitchen piled high with last night's mess?

Are you trying to do school while your two-year-old climbs all over you, on the schoolbooks, and interrupts continuously?

Do you wonder why your nine-year-old son continues to struggle with spelling?

Are you totally frustrated with yourself because you responded with irritation toward your child?

Is it "that time of the month"?

Is your husband ungrateful for all you do?

You can easily add your personal situations to this list. It doesn't take much evaluation of our interactions in life to quickly determine what it is that robs us of our meek and quiet spirit.

Three Categories

As we study the list of meek and quiet spirit robbers, I think they fall into three main categories: fear, disorganization, and anger. Each of these is the opposite of a meek and quiet spirit. These negative characteristics keep us from teaching (and loving) our children as we so greatly desire.

Are we helpless victims of our emotions? Do our feelings have to rule our lives and leave us forever at odds with a meek and quiet spirit? I believe the Lord offers great hope in our quest to teach with a meek and quiet spirit. In the next chapters, we'll take each of these areas (fear, disorganization, and anger) and see which real-life, practical aids we can apply to them. In addition, we will look at some proactive things we can do to facilitate a meek and quiet spirit. For now, read the following application projects, and get started!

Application Projects

1. Begin a list to record every time you sense you are not exhibiting a meek and quiet spirit.

2. Write out a prayer to the Lord concerning your heart's desire to homeschool with a meek and quiet spirit.

3. Start looking for Scripture verses that will support having a meek and quiet spirit.

Chapter Two

Undergirding

When I am first introduced to another mom, I never tell her two things about me unless she inquires point-blank. The answers to these two questions she might ask are often overwhelming. Immediately, the conversation takes a directed turn. What are the two answers? We have eight children and homeschool!

Usually the next statement in the conversation is, "Oh my! You must be the most patient woman in the world! I could never do that! My two children drive me crazy!" I am at a loss as to how to reply. I am certainly not the most patient woman in the world. In fact, patience would be one of my least natural characteristics. In addition, my children are very normal, active, strong-willed children–all of them! I have sometimes teased Steve, my husband, that it would have been nice if we could have had some "followers" rather than eight "leaders."

I have pondered this "other mom's" thoughts and asked the Lord what difference has come about in my own life to make me happy to have eight children and homeschool. The answer is the whole undergirding of a meek and quiet spirit.

Meeting with the Lord

For the past fifteen years of my twenty-four-year walk with the Lord Jesus, He has shown me the importance of spending daily time with Him in His Word and in prayer. It has become a commitment from my heart that I would begin my day by getting up early enough to spend time with Him.

Most homeschooling moms start their homeschooling journey with a definite call from the Lord to homeschool, whether it is through their husband's direction or simply a burden on their own heart. They are stepping out in faith as they start to homeschool, knowing that in no way are they "qualified" or "capable" of homeschooling. However, they are convinced that their God is bigger than any of their failings, and they cling joyously to 2 Corinthians 12:9, "And he said unto me, My grace is sufficient for thee: for my strength is made perfect in weakness. Most gladly therefore will I rather glory in my infirmities, that the power of Christ may rest upon me." They believe the truth of Philippians 4:13, "I can do all things through Christ which strengtheneth me."

As the busyness of homeschooling days becomes routine, what is often the first "expendable" activity to be dropped from Mom's day? Unfortunately, but truthfully, it is usually spending time alone with the Lord. Following is a note that shares a common experience among homeschooling moms:

"Today I was thinking about why my days have been so bad lately. I realized that I have not been having my quiet

time with the Lord in the morning. I have been lying in bed justifying that I need the sleep more than I need the time alone. Then I realized, if I'm faithful to get up in the morning and spend time with Him, He will provide strength for me throughout the day (in a way that extra hour of sleep never could)." Kelly in TX

The key to our meek and quiet spirit is time with the Lord Jesus Christ. However, we think we need those few extra minutes of sleep to help us through the day rather than rising when the alarm goes off. Our need is not for sleep, although it is important to assure we are getting adequate rest. Our need is for the empowering that comes through intimacy with the One Who called us to the task of home educating.

I am not saying these private hours with Jesus are some kind of "magic pill" that will ward off all my troubles. Rather, it is that special meeting with my God where I learn of Him and pour my heart out to Him. It is the key to growing close to my Lord and having my spirit renewed each day.

Martha or Mary?

Here is a story I believe we can all relate to and learn greatly from. Luke 10:38-42, "Now it came to pass, as they went, that he entered into a certain village: and a certain woman named Martha received him into her house. And she had a sister called Mary, which also sat at Jesus' feet, and heard his word. But Martha was cumbered about much serving, and came to him, and said, Lord, dost thou not care that my sister hath left me to serve alone? bid her therefore that she help me. And Jesus answered and said unto her, Martha, Martha, thou art careful and troubled about many things: But one thing is needful: and Mary hath chosen that good part, which shall not be taken away from her."

I have long wondered how many homeschooling moms would classify themselves as a "Martha" and how many as a "Mary." I expected we would tip the balance on the "Martha" side. One day, in a workshop I was giving to about one hundred and fifty homeschooling moms, I took a poll. When I asked how many moms saw themselves as "Martha," it seemed like all the hands in the room went up. As I asked for the "Marys" I realized why it appeared all hands had raised with the first question. They had–except for the one that rose as a "Mary"!

We are busy being Martha. We are pushing to finish our daily schoolwork, keep up with the laundry, do the chores, and put meals on the table. The list can be unending. There is much to do, and it is all very important. Will we heed the voice of Jesus telling us that only one thing is "needful"? Despite how we feel about what we are accomplishing and what we are not getting to, the one "needful" thing is our time with Him.

Here is a note I received from a mother of ten children, ages fourteen and down.

"I have discovered the source of my discouragement. My problem is that I was not spending any quiet time with the Lord. I haven't for years. I wasn't drawing near to Him, and I had conceded that all of my homeschooling friends had the same problems that I had. We were just burned out and overburdened. I now have scheduled 'tea time with the Lord' in my day, first thing." Marilyn

We make choices as to how we will spend our time. If a meek and quiet spirit is truly a great desire of our hearts, then we will discover that we must do what Jesus Himself told us was "needful"–spend time with Him.

I know there were plenty of other activities I could have done over the past fifteen years during that half-hour to hour a day I spent with the Lord. We could have done more schooling, had a cleaner house, more fun playtimes, more ministry, more individual time with each child, more writing, more sewing, better meals, more exercise, or more sleep! I look back over those years and all the choices set before me as to how to use those hours. I know there is nothing that could have had the impact on my life, and the lives of my family members, than time with the Lord. This is particularly true in the realm of a meek and quiet spirit. Any other decision for that time would have been one more robber of a meek and quiet spirit. However, time with the Lord is the opposite. It was the one "needful" thing for me. It was a meek and quiet spirit builder!

Encouragement from the Word

Consider, for a moment, a few Scriptures to encourage us in our need for this daily time with the Lord. Psalm 119:105, "Thy word is a lamp unto my feet, and a light unto my path." Don't we desire to know the way the Lord has prepared for us personally and for each of our children? Have you heard, or even said yourself, "If the Lord would just send a letter telling me what to do in this situation, I would be so happy to obey!" God has sent us much more than a letter; He has given us a whole book! The more we root and ground ourselves in His Word, the more we will understand His will in choices we must make. We can face these decisions with a meek and quiet spirit: "And be not conformed to this world: but be ye transformed by the renewing of your mind, that ye may prove what is that good, and acceptable, and perfect, will of God" (Romans 12:2).

"But we have this treasure in earthen vessels, that the excellency of the power may be of God, and not of us. We are troubled on every side, yet not distressed; we are perplexed, but not in despair; Persecuted, but not forsaken; cast down, but not destroyed" (2 Corinthians 4:7-8). Does this describe the way you feel some days? So how is it that we "that the excellency of the power may be of God, and not of us" if we don't have time in our day to spend with God? Without daily reliance on Jesus Christ, aren't we working through our day in our own power and strength? Won't we muddle along without a meek and quiet spirit?

"All scripture is given by inspiration of God, and is profitable for doctrine, for reproof, for correction, for instruction in righteous: That the man of God may be perfect, thoroughly furnished unto all good works" (2 Timothy 3:16-17). Isn't this another of our heart's desires, to be thoroughly equipped for every good work the Lord has for us to do and especially in the teaching of our children? If we don't spend time daily with the Lord in His Word, will this be possible?

My heart desperately needs the Word of God every single day! I have a scheduled time early in the morning to pray, read my Bible, and memorize Scripture. For the most part this keeps me consistent, but occasionally we are up quite late at night. This can impact my time with the Lord the next morning. I wonder if my family can tell the days I have really met with Him versus the ones I hurry through my reading, prayer, and memory time or skip it altogether. They don't ask me that question, but perhaps on days when my irritation is quick to show through, it would be good accountability for me if they did.

When my youngest child was a baby, she went through a stage when she wasn't nursing well at her breakfast time feeding. We decided that I should quit waking her up at 5:30 a.m. to nurse so she would be hungrier at 8:30 a.m. As we began doing this, I found I became very nervous from 6:45 until 7:45 because I would not be available if she happened to wake up and be hungry. I was out of the house, walking, and someone at home would have to pacify her if she awakened. That time became miserable for me because of my anxiety over the baby. I asked Steve, and he agreed that we could go back to waking the baby up early in the morning. Do you know what happened? Rather than dreading having to get up at 5:30 every morning to nurse the baby, I loved it. I was so happy to again have a peaceful heart during that hour I was out walking that I didn't mind, in the least, the early morning nursing time.

In a similar way, our time feasting on the Word should be so important to us that we don't care a bit that we are rising earlier than we might otherwise, or that we are taking quiet afternoon time when the children sleep to meet with the Lord.

Prayer

Philippians 4:6 says, "Be careful for nothing; but in every thing by prayer and supplication with thanksgiving let your requests be made known unto God. And the peace of God, which passeth all understanding, shall keep your hearts and minds through Christ Jesus." Here again, we can immediately see the application of our time alone with the Lord, each day, in setting the stage for our meek and quiet spirits.

"My voice shalt thou hear in the morning, O Lord; in the morning will I direct my prayer unto thee, and will look up." (Psalm 5:3). Do you? Do I? Or do we only take the time to shoot up flare prayers during each crisis that occurs throughout the day. Is this truly laying our requests before God, or is it asking Him to be a firefighter for us? How can you keep a record of God's answers to prayer in your life, and your family's lives, if you don't have a consistent time to spend in prayer alone?

Have you noticed how much more of an intimate conversation you can have with your husband when the two of you are alone and have each other's undivided attention? Once, when Steve and I were able to get away together for a weekend, we were so amazed at how far we could get in a conversation with no interruptions! It is the same with our prayer time. Undisturbed time for prayer is the basis of our hearts and minds being kept through Christ Jesus–truly a meek and quiet spirit! "But thou, when thou prayest, enter into thy closet, and when thou hast shut thy door, pray to thy Father which is in secret ..." (Matthew 6:6).

Undergirding Foundation

There is an important very first step in developing a meek and quiet spirit that I don't want to assume is in place in each homeschooling mom's life. There will be no fruit from personal time with Jesus until you actually have a relationship with Him. For many years of my life, I believed I was a Christian. I attended church on Sunday. That was the basis for labeling myself as a Christian. However, church was as far as my intimacy with Jesus went. There was no day-to-day interaction with Him except for a regular commitment on Sunday to work harder at doing what I thought I ought to be doing.

Not long after Steve and I were married, while still in college, we began attending a small church in our college community. Steve had met the pastor, a very sound biblical preacher, at the radio station where he worked. This was a radio station aimed at college students. However, because of financial need, they allowed this pastor to purchase a daily half-hour time slot, when the students were mostly in class.

Steve would work on equipment and listen to the Bible being taught. He was challenged by what he heard and even began to ask the preacher some questions. Steve was amazed that the preacher never gave his own thoughts in answer but would always reply, "Right here in the Bible, it says ..." Soon we were visiting this church.

While we determined to fit in with the crowd calling the others "Brother" and "Sister," it became evident to both Steve and I that we were not, as they would say, "saved." This was a new term to us, but we didn't sit under biblical teaching long before we learned what it meant.

It took a while longer for us to become convinced that thinking we were Christians was not enough to qualify as being "saved." I believed I hadn't been too "bad" and certainly didn't see myself as a sinner. I really thought I was as good as most other people and much better than many! As far as the faults I did have, I just needed to try a little harder.

A verse that was instrumental in our change of thought was James 2:19, which says, "Thou believest that there is one God; thou doest well: the devils also believe, and tremble." We came to realize that the devils' belief was simply an understanding of a fact. They knew the fact that Jesus was God, but knowing that fact does not save a person. Salvation requires repentance and life-changing faith in Jesus' death, burial, and resurrection. Salvation means making Jesus the Lord of my life.

The following verses were instrumental in bringing me to a saving knowledge of Jesus Christ. They pointed out my own sinful condition and the consequences of that sin. They also showed me that I wasn't able to try hard enough to be good. Salvation was a gift of God that came to me through His grace. I had to first believe it, and then act on it.

Romans 3:23, "For all have sinned, and come short of the glory of God."

Romans 6:23, "For the wages of sin is death; but the gift of God is eternal life through Jesus Christ our Lord."

Romans 5:8-10, "But God commendeth his love toward us, in that, while we were yet sinners, Christ died for us. Much more then, being now justified by his blood, we shall be saved from wrath through him. For if, when we were enemies, we were reconciled to God by the death of his Son, much more, being reconciled, we shall be saved by his life."

Romans 10:9-10, "That if thou shalt confess with thy mouth the Lord Jesus, and shalt believe in thine heart that God hath raised him from the dead, thou shalt be saved. For with the heart man believeth unto righteousness; and with the mouth confession is made unto salvation."

Ephesians 2:8-9, "For by grace are ye saved through faith; and that not of yourselves: it is the gift of God: Not of works, lest any man should boast."

Within a few short weeks of each other, both Steve and I did exactly what Romans 10:9-10 says. We saw ourselves as sinners in desperate need of a Savior. Then we confessed Jesus with our mouths, believing in our hearts that God had raised Him from the dead.

I encourage you to consider for yourself whether you have followed Scripture and truly have a personal relationship with Jesus Christ. This is the very beginning of a meek and quiet spirit.

Undergirding Foundation How-To

Just in case there are any readers who don't know how to go about spending time with the Lord, please let me give you some ideas. Sometimes a mom will avoid daily time in the Word simply because she doesn't know what to do. Since your relationship with Jesus Christ grows out of your knowledge of Him, it is vital that you plan time with Him and use those hours wisely.

First, it is important that you schedule a time each day to spend in prayer and Bible reading. How much time you take for this will depend on you and your circumstances. Personally, I schedule a minimum of a half-hour a day and a maximum of an hour. Find a time in your day when you can reliably be committed to these devotions. If you are up with a nursing baby in the night, you might find that early afternoon, when the baby naps and you are awake, is better than early mornings. Whatever the scheduled time, keep it as a priority!

Plan to read your Bible each day. Devotionals are nice and easy to read. However, I encourage you to be in the Word for yourself, at least a chapter's worth. Dig out and find your own applications. I like to record what I read each day, plus copy out one verse that has personal meaning to me. Then I take it a step further and write out why I chose that verse. It may be that I need to grow in the area it is teaching. It could be that I want to meditate throughout the day on that particular characteristic of God.

A prayer journal is important too. I have been so embarrassed, on occasion, to have a friend thank me for praying, only to have to admit I completely forgot to pray for her need. It is absolutely awful! My prayer journal has been a helpful tool to remind me to pray for things that are certainly very important to me, but which I tend to forget when other things press in on my mind.

I am currently using a small, prettily bound, blank-page book for my prayer journal. I write in the date, the prayer request, and leave two blank lines for answers. When a prayer is answered, I write it in my prayer journal and check the request off. Then I can tell at a glance what I want to pray about on each page. Some pages get completely checked off with time; others have ongoing needs that are open ended.

There is no right way, or wrong way, to spend your Bible and prayer time. I share what I like to do simply because I am sure there are women who don't spend time with the Lord because they don't know what to do.

Much of what our hearts yearn for, in our homes, is tied back to this very special time. If you have felt the Lord's call to teach in your homeschool with a meek and quiet spirit, but have been neglecting to seek Him daily by setting aside a time to spend alone with Him, may I strongly encourage you to not let another day go by before you remedy this situation. May we each follow Marilyn's example and begin our day with "tea time with the Lord"!

Application Projects

1. Schedule a daily time to spend reading your Bible and praying. Begin right away!

2. Purchase a notebook for your Bible reading notes and one for a prayer journal. You could also use a tabbed notebook and have them together.

3. Start using the notebook to help with your time with the Lord.

4. Find a friend who would like to be encouraged by regularly having a personal devotion each day as well. Agree to hold each other accountable.

Chapter Three

Fear and Worry

2 Timothy 1:7 states, "For God hath not given us the spirit of fear; but of power, and of love, and of a sound mind." Yet, how often do we find our meek and quiet spirit disturbed by fear? Perhaps you are concerned about your ability to actually facilitate the education of your child. Maybe you are worried about your curriculum choices. It could be you are feeling that your daily example to your children is not good for them. There are many areas of our homeschooling lives that can be bombarded by fears. How do we combat these?

Don't Change Course!

Begin by recalling how you were led to your home-schooling adventure in the first place. Few will homeschool without the knowledge that this is God's direction for their family. Keep in mind that the Lord uses difficulties in what we are doing to refine and grow us. Seldom are those struggles a signal to undo what He has called us to do! The problems should be pulling us to a greater level of seeking the

Lord and depending on Him. They should not be causing us to consider returning to where we were before He directed us to homeschool.

Mentally recall some of the best-known Bible stories. In many of them, a godly man is given a specific task from the Lord. This person soon faces difficulties. Are these obstacles circumstances from the Lord to change His follower's direction? We know, without a doubt, that they are not. Yet, in our lives, we will question our homeschooling "call" when we face trials.

Do you remember the story of Daniel when he was no longer allowed to pray to God three times a day, but rather he could only bow down to the king? Were Daniel's difficulties a sign from God to stop his habit of daily prayer or an opportunity to deepen his trust and reliance on God? In a similar way, I challenge us to use any struggles we have in homeschooling as a springboard to grow in our faith. May we never choose to turn back from the path the Lord has set us upon simply because it isn't easy.

Captive Thoughts

We have such a great opportunity to teach our children the right responses to difficulties. They are very aware of our struggles and emotions, particularly when it comes to fears and worries. We can choose to follow what 2 Corinthians 10:5 says, "Casting down imaginations, and every high thing that exalteth itself against the knowledge of God, and bringing into captivity every thought to the obedience of Christ," by not allowing ourselves to dwell on our concerns. When we don't let our minds dwell on those concerns, we gain the benefit of maintaining a meek and quiet spirit through a distressing situation. Moreover, we show our children what it truly means to rest in the Lord!

For example, when I become too busy, I am quite prone to being fearful and worrying. If I allow my mind to mull on what has to be done, I feel totally overwhelmed. I want to run and hide, not even trying to do anything. Rather than doing that, though, I push myself into overdrive. This causes me to be short and irritable with my family. I become unhappy as well.

If I make the choice to take my thoughts captive, busyness becomes a vehicle to greater resting in the Lord. I can remind myself that the Lord has not called me to do more than there is time for. He desires the fruit of the Spirit in my life, not fear, worry, frustration, and irritation. The joy of the Lord is my strength. I can pray when the fears and worries attack, asking the Lord for direction on how to use my time and which activities should have the highest priority. Even if everything isn't accomplished that I think should be, it is so much better to go to bed at night being behind in what needs to be done than to go to bed angry and upset.

My children are very aware of my reactions to what is going on around me. They may see me push to get things done while wronging those I love with my attitudes and maybe my actions as well. On the other hand, they may see me walk though times of stress with a meek and quiet spirit.

Your Special Scripture

If the Lord didn't put a Scripture on your heart when you began to homeschool, seek Him for one now. During my early years of homeschooling, I struggled greatly with times of depression. I was encouraged to pray for a special Scripture promise from the Lord just for my homeschooling. I did that, and let me share with you the verses the Lord put on my heart one day as I was reading them in my quiet time with Him.

Isaiah 44:3-5, "For I will pour water upon him that is thirsty, and floods upon the dry ground: I will pour my spirit upon thy seed, and my blessing upon thine offspring: And they shall spring up as among the grass, as willows by the water courses. One shall say, I am the Lord's; and another shall call himself by the name of Jacob; and another shall subscribe with his hand unto the Lord, and surname himself by the name of Israel."

These verses were such a relief to me. The outcome of our homeschooling was not my responsibility! The Lord Himself was involved in this process with a stake in the results. When depression overcame me, my thoughts would become very unreasonable. Quoting this verse to myself was a lifeline to the truth that my mind could not think on its own. Recalling Scripture is a part of "bringing into captivity every thought to the obedience of Christ."

Our Weapon

Prayer is such a mighty weapon for us to use as we battle to replace fear, worry, and insecurity with a meek and quiet spirit. Rather than giving in to these emotions, let's learn to turn each fear and worry into a request given to God with thanksgiving. "Be careful for nothing; but in every thing by prayer and supplication with thanksgiving let your requests be made known unto God" (Philippians 4:6).

I have greatly treasured my younger children's naptime in the afternoon, especially when my five little ones were ages seven and under. Those two hours of quiet were my time to regroup and refresh for the rest of the day. Often, I found myself fearful that the baby would awaken in the middle of naptime. This would spoil my sewing or rest time.

Finally, I realized I needed to make this a matter of prayer rather than being so fearful. I asked the Lord to help me accept it if the baby awoke early. I prepared myself to give up my personal plans in order to care for the baby, knowing that the Lord was the One Who ultimately determined whether the baby slept or awoke.

Steve and I pray about each school year's curriculum decisions. For several years, I found that after we had prayerfully made a decision together, I would reconsider it, weighing it over and over in my mind. Soon I doubted the choices we had made, and I was trapped in fears and worries over our curriculum.

I had to make a conscious effort to remember that the decisions had been made based on our joint discussions and prayer ("bringing into captivity every thought to the obedience of Christ"). These decisions were not something for me to be rethinking in the first place, let alone placing myself above the Lord's leading and my husband's direction.

Steve and I will frequently make a curriculum choice that isn't what most homeschoolers are using. We make our decisions based on what we discern to be the Lord's leading, particularly considering the spiritual needs of our children. We realize that the Lord is very capable of filling any academic gaps that might exist in the curriculum we choose. Basing decisions on prayer is a powerful ally in dispelling fears and helping to teach with a meek and quiet spirit.

The Lord, the Teacher

Consider with me Isaiah 54:13, "And all thy children shall be taught of the Lord; and great shall be the peace of thy children." I am one who believes strongly in the need for homeschooling mothers to take quite seriously their moral and legal obligation to truly "school" their children. However, in looking at this verse, we can see Who is actually doing the teaching. What a joy! When that fear creeps in, we can combat it by remembering ("bringing into captivity every thought to the obedience of Christ") that the

Lord is working on our behalf teaching our children. We are taking our thoughts captive.

At times when my adult children want to control their younger siblings, I like to share this thought with them. It is much easier to be the person who carries out the "orders" than to be the one who makes them. They really don't want the added responsibility that goes with controlling the little ones. In a very similar way, when I can view myself as simply following the Lord's orders, then I don't have to own the responsibility for the outcome. When this is true, many of the fears and worries vanish.

It may be that you have begun your six-year-old on a phonics program, but it is going poorly at best. You start to worry that the phonics program was not a wise investment, or that your child has some kind of learning disability. How can you regain a meek and quiet spirit in this situation? You take your thoughts captive and remember several things.

First, you prayed about your choice of a phonics program, and the Lord led you to this one. Secondly, much is learned in homeschooling aside from the actual targeted "academics." Perhaps the Lord has in mind some other learning through this problem.

Maybe this is an opportunity for your child to learn to persevere through something that doesn't come easily for him. It could be that this is a time for you to develop added patience while you gently and sweetly work with your child each day, even though the progress isn't visible. Rather than giving in to fear or worry, spend time with the Lord and your husband discerning if there are "bigger" learning projects in this trial than a six-year-old who isn't "getting it." Face your concerns with a meek and quiet spirit!

Godly Sorrow or Worldly Sorrow

Very often, our biggest fears and insecurities stem from doubts about our personal influence on our children. This happens in light of our ongoing and regular failures. If we fail, become irritated, are angry, or show poor self-discipline in any area, we are painfully aware of how quickly the children pick up our sins, mirroring them back to us.

"On days like this, I wonder why I, of all people, have been blessed with children because they deserve better." Nancy

2 Corinthians 7:9-10 says, "Now I rejoice, not that ye were made sorry, but that ye sorrowed to repentance: for ye were made sorry after a godly manner, that ye might receive damage by us in nothing. For godly sorrow worketh repentance to salvation not to be repented of: but the sorrow of the world worketh death." While this verse seems to be speaking about salvation, it gave me some thoughts about the difference between worldly sorrow and godly sorrow.

Unfortunately, in my life, I am prone to worldly sorrow; perhaps in your life, you are as well. Although I don't want to admit it, it stems from a twisted measure of pride. It thinks, "I have failed again. Won't this ever change? I am such a negative example to my children. They would be better off away from me all day! I have prayed and prayed, tried and tried, but here I am again!"

Godly sorrow, on the other hand, knows that as 1 John 1:9 says, "If we confess our sins, he is faithful and just to forgive us our sins, and to cleanse us from all unrighteousness." It also believes Romans 8:1, "There is therefore now no condemnation to them which are in Christ Jesus, who walk not after the flesh, but after the Spirit."

Remember my son who takes so much of my time and energy for his homeschooling? It is very easy for me to have a frustrated tone in my voice when I am interacting with him. The Lord will convict me of this. When I respond with worldly sorrow, here is how my thinking goes, "This child is just more than I can handle patiently. I am not cut out for this task. I have prayed for patience. I have worked at being meek with him, but I keep failing over and over." My whole focus is on me. I have no real concern for this particular sin in my life. My sorrow is worldly because it wants to be right and good on its own efforts.

This is how I see godly sorrow handling the same situation, "Lord, You have said that man's anger does not bring about the righteous life that You desire. You have also said that love is patient and kind. I have not been obedient to You. Your fruit is not showing forth to my son. I am wrong, Lord. Please forgive me. Thank you for your forgiveness and working in my life. I submit myself to You and ask you to continue to teach me Your ways." Then I quickly confess my wrong attitudes and tone of voice to my son and ask his forgiveness.

Godly sorrow truly grieves over sin, confesses, and repents of it. Then godly sorrow puts a smile on its face and walks in the joy of "no condemnation!" Every day I have the opportunity to teach my children to react to their sin with godly sorrow or worldly sorrow. I make the decision myself, conscious or not, as to whether I will be filled with self-pity and worry over my sin, or whether I will submit it properly to the Lord and move on ("bringing into captivity every thought to the obedience of Christ").

Follow Your Husband

Another aspect of overcoming the fears that steal our meek and quiet spirit rests on our ability to truly trust our husband's leadership and words. Some Christian home-schooling moms do not have a husband who will give them direction, but most do. Learn to take your fears and worries to your husband. Get his counsel and then follow it, whether he is a Christian or not! If he says you are making too big a deal, believe him!

It is most likely when a Christian family begins to homeschool that both the husband and wife are in agreement that this is the Lord's direction for the family. When homeschool becomes difficult, I encourage you, Mom, never to consider quitting unless your husband is the one who says you are to do so.

Keep in mind: it is entirely possible that a loving husband, one who does not want his wife to "suffer," might suggest she quit homeschooling even though he wishes her to continue. This will usually be the result of the wife having regularly complained about her struggles, fears, and failures. Eventually, despite his heart's desire, the husband will decide homeschooling is just too much for his wife. Therefore, consider well the possible consequences of not developing a meek and quiet spirit.

Let me share a story with you about how the Lord began to teach me to trust that my husband will point out real faults in my life. There was a time in my life when I struggled and struggled with thinking I was overweight. In reality, I was not overweight, but in my perception of myself I was. My thoughts about my weight ended up affecting how I dealt with my days in general, giving me an overall feeling of being unhappy. Finally, one day, the Lord spoke to my heart. He caused me to think about what difference it made if I was overweight except perhaps to my husband. At that point, I decided to accept my weight where it was unless my husband began to tell me I needed to lose weight.

In a similar way, we are often too hard on ourselves. Areas of my life that I think are not right are often only my own misperceptions. The man who knows me best, my husband, does not see a problem. I need to learn to trust God to use my husband to show me my failures, particularly if I am prone to worldly sorrow rather than godly sorrow.

Instead of fearing you are failing in an aspect of your homeschooling, trust that if you truly are failing, your husband will become aware of it and point it out.

Husbands can also help allay fear and worry concerning curriculum decisions if we will bring these decisions to him to help make. I will often discuss potential curriculum with Steve. I sometimes write out the information he needs to know to help with the decision. I do this because I know he is not aware of how the curriculums work in their day-to-day usage in our homeschool. Having the facts before him allows him to pray and think before we make a final decision.

I remember a time we were choosing a new curriculum. I had read and mulled over a sample of a curriculum I thought had potential. I had poured over it for hours and was praying about it. Finally, I showed an area of slight concern in the curriculum to Steve. Within one minute, he had told me that the curriculum was not for us! All that wasted energy on my part. Had I taken the curriculum to him earlier, I could have bypassed so much of that thinking time.

(Update: since this book was written, I have begun giving a session called *Loving Your Husband*. In it, I encourage you to develop and strengthen your relationship with your husband, and I share many personal examples. For more information on the CD, see www.Titus2.com.)

Who We Are

Consider with me one more aspect of fear and worry as a meek and quiet spirit robber. For most women, monthly hormonal changes cause some days to be filled with emotions that are not a part of other days. The same is true when we are tired. Nothing looks positive if we are overly tired. Our fears are exaggerated; we find things to worry about when there is nothing to worry about at all.

Hormonal ups and downs are a part of the way the Lord made us. Coming to terms with the fact that they have an influence on our emotions will go a long way toward helping us live with them. We will be much better off if we pray through these days, rather than allow our emotions to rule our behavior. Try to run on "autopilot," not reacting or responding to anything but waiting until a day when the hormonal emotions have passed.

Learn to recognize the signs in your life of being tired. Here might be a few: crying easily, becoming angry over situations that don't normally bother you, feeling like nothing is right, having no energy, or feeling overwhelmed. When you are tired, commit to being very quiet, pray constantly, and get to bed as soon as possible. Don't make any major decisions, and certainly don't dwell on any areas that are troubling to you. Just get some sleep.

Dealing with our fears and worries is a big part of a meek and quiet spirit. Being aware of fears as they enter our minds, and then facing them as Scripture tells us to, can keep us from becoming their victims. Rather, as we rest in the sovereignty, goodness, and trustworthiness of our Lord, we can walk through fears and uncertainties with a meek and quiet spirit.

Application Projects

1. Begin to write down each time you are fearful or worried about something.

2. Look for Scriptures that would combat the fear or worry so that you can take your thoughts captive to the obedience of Christ. Write the verses down for reference as needed.

3. Make a list of what the Lord could want to teach you through each situation that is causing you to fear or worry.

4. Start praying for a special Scripture for your homeschool.

5. The next time you doubt your positive influence on your children, evaluate whether you are experiencing godly sorrow or worldly sorrow.

6. Ask your husband for his insights about the situation when you are fearful or worried.

7. Write down your personal signs of being tired or having hormonal fluctuations.

Chapter Four

Disorganization

For many of us, our meek and quiet spirit flees when: our laundry piles up, things are out all over the place, the kitchen is a mess, the closets and drawers are disaster, and the children or our husbands won't pick up! The list of irritations caused by disorganization is unending and very personal. Most moms simply function better in a neat, orderly home. Many fewer have actually achieved this! I have yet to talk to a mom who is not more content when her home is nice and tidy.

"I had the house completely clean two days ago, and now it is a disaster. Some times it feels like, why clean it if this is what happens?" Gwynette

"I used to be an extremely poor housekeeper (slob would be a better word!) and though I don't love housecleaning now, I do enjoy a clean house. I do have days where I will leave dishes in the sink overnight, or leave messes out or laundry unwashed or unfolded, but usually if I can keep the house picked up, the 'deep cleaning' can be let go longer, and no one really notices. Nobody notices if the floor isn't done once

a week, everyone notices if there are no clean dishes or no clean clothes." Nan

Time

It seems to me that there are few organizational issues that can't be solved if a mom gives time to them. Think about it. If your child's room is cluttered, you are the only one who knows the size of the bedroom, the closet, and the other furniture in that room. If you were to spend a day working in that room, looking at it, and praying for solutions to the particular clutter difficulties, you could probably come up with some great ideas.

Usually, though, our organization problems end up at the bottom of the time priority list and at the top of the meek and quiet spirit robbers' list. It may be because they have grown so out-of-hand there seems to be no light at the end of the tunnel. The thinking then is, "Why even bother to begin?" It is possible we have filled our days so full of other activities that time for organization has been totally left out. Perhaps we have given some of our day to organization issues but not enough to keep up with it.

Giving the needed time to your particular organizational problems will be very effective toward their solutions. Schedule a part of your day—an hour would be ideal, but thirty minutes can be effective too—to work on organization difficulties. When your scheduled time is up, stop right where you are. Begin again the next day where you left off.

Know what to tackle first by developing a prioritized list of the areas that "bug" you the most. These will be the ones that are negatively affecting your meek and quiet spirit.

Using your schedule to help with any of your organizational challenges should be beneficial. Simply schedule time so you can work on those specific areas. If there isn't time in your schedule, then accept the fact that these issues aren't that big. If they aren't a high enough priority to invest time in, they certainly aren't important enough to steal a meek and quiet spirit! If they are causing you distress, you may have to go back to your husband and the Lord to reevaluate your time usage.

Your daily schedule will help, in general, with organizational issues. If you have time scheduled for laundry, it won't be piling up. Scheduling housecleaning helps assure that chores are not falling behind. A time slot for deskwork keeps the paper clutter from becoming preposterous. Each of these small areas has the potential of robbing you of a meek and quiet spirit. While this loss has little effect on the laundry, housecleaning, or paperwork, it does take its toll on our families!

Let me share with you a note I received that should help convince you of the benefits of scheduling organizational time into your day. This comment refers to the book *Managers of Their Homes: A Practical Guide to Daily Scheduling for Christian Home-School Families*, which my husband and I have written for homeschooling families on how to schedule.

> *"The very next day, following our prayer, Managers of Their Homes arrived in the mail. My first reaction was negative, 'my life is too chaotic to be THAT rigid,' but as I began to read, I realized my life was too chaotic because I WASN'T scheduled. I was driven by the tyranny of the urgent. So many things were being left undone because something else seemed more pressing.*

> *One of my favorite suggestions the Maxwells share in the book is the thirty-minute principle. Do a given task for thirty minutes, and when your time is up, put it away until the next day.*

> *Immediately, I applied this to a box of 'stuff' in my kitchen, which I'd been tripping over since Christmas. Most horizontal surfaces in my home invite paper, books, Lego's—whatever needs a place to stay away from its given home. Christmas Day I cleared one of these horizontal surfaces (the top of my portable dishwasher) into a cardboard box with the intention to take care of the 'stuff' later.*

> *I dreaded that box!! Every day I'd think, 'I'd better take care of that box,' only to put it off until the next day. After reading the 'thirty-minute' rule, I got up from the book, set the timer for thirty minutes and went to work. It was almost finished by the end, but I closed the box and didn't return to it until the next day. It took only fifteen minutes*

to finish, which gave me fifteen minutes to do something else.

My box no longer plagues my mind. I'm accomplishing many 'put off' chores in my thirty-minute-a-day method. I feel I'm redeeming my time now rather than time controlling me." Susan

May I encourage you that losing a meek and quiet spirit to organization issues just isn't worth it. Push yourself to get started in those areas for that set amount of time. When your "timer" goes off, put it away, and pick it up the next day. For more detailed information on scheduling for home-schoolers, our book, *Managers of Their Homes*, would be useful. (Ordering information on *Managers of Their Homes* can be found in the back of this book.)

Husband's Solutions

Discussing organizational obstacles with your husband and seeking his ideas for solutions will be helpful. He knows you, your home, and your situation better than anyone else. You might be quite surprised by his quick, brilliant solution to a problem that has been plaguing you!

I remember struggling, for several months, with a schoolbook case. The books left in the bookcase kept falling over each time we removed the ones we were going to use. Once the remaining books toppled, it was hard to replace the "in use" books back into the bookcase when we were finished with them. I explained my problem to Steve.

"Simple," he said, "I can easily build dividers on the shelves." He did just that, and we haven't had a problem since.

Master Lists

Master lists can be an immense help in solving organization problems. Having a master grocery list, a master warehouse shopping list (SAMS, Costco), and a master meals list will save you great amounts of time. You will not be writing "milk" every week on your grocery list; it will already be there. All you must do is fill in how many gallons you want.

There was a time I could make out my grocery list without even entering the kitchen. My memory was good enough that I knew how many eggs we had, how much flour was left, and what the veggie status was. With added gray hair and a daughter who helps greatly in the kitchen, I now have no idea how much we have of anything!

My master grocery list has saved us many unnecessary trips to the grocery store, in addition to helping maintain my meek and quiet spirit. On that master grocery list are the items I usually buy every week at the grocery store. My list is kept on the computer so I can print it out each week, but you could make a master grocery list by hand. If you do it by hand, you could photocopy several months' worth at a time.

I take that master grocery list into our kitchen and look to see the status of each item on the list. I mark beside it whether to purchase, and if so, how many or how much.

There is also room on the list to add ingredients and food we don't buy every week. My master grocery list has a place for me to write in the meals I have scheduled for the week. This helps me remember to put the ingredients for these meals on the master grocery list.

I post the menu on the refrigerator, because I might not recall what I had planned for a meal as the week progresses. This posting of the meal plan also helps me with a meek and quiet spirit because family members can see the upcoming meals. I'm not plagued with the "what's for dinner?" question. If they don't like the meal, they have some time to get used to the idea!

My master grocery list is available on our web site, www.Titus2.com. It could be that looking at someone else's master grocery list will spur you on as to how you can make one designed to meet your family's specific needs.

Master Donut List

Let me share with you some other master lists so that you might begin thinking in these terms yourself. A handful of times a year, Steve will say that we are going to have donuts for breakfast. Great excitement abounds in the Maxwell household over a special breakfast such as this. However, next Dad inquires, "Now what does everyone want?" You can't imagine the pandemonium that breaks out with nine people wanting to know what their choices are, how many donuts they get, and finally shouting their order at Daddy. Daddy does have a "donut limit"! In this situation, it could be pushed to the point where he would say, "Never mind. It isn't worth it!"

One morning, after a particularly trying time of gathering the donut order, we made up a "Master Donut Order," and typed it on the computer. Now all we have to do is pull it up, print it, and send it with the one who is going to the grocery store. SIMPLE!

Master Vacation Lists

Have you noticed that preparing for a vacation is one of those times that can rob you of a meek and quiet spirit? Try master lists!

In recent years, we have begun vacationing in the same place. The first year Steve and I spent significant time discussing and deciding what to take to eat and how much of it. I saved the menu plans for the next year. That second trip, I took it a step further. I noted what we wished we had had and what was too much. Now I have a master vacation meal and shopping list. I can customize it for each trip, but I don't have to start from scratch!

I did the same thing with our vacation-packing list. Steve and I both had handwritten lists we had generated to help us not forget anything. After the trip, I typed them on the computer and saved them. I added a few items we would have liked to have had with us and eliminated a few we didn't need. What a time saver that will be when we get ready to go again!

Tools

Finally, in the area of organization, save toward and invest in organizational and storage solutions and tools. Ask other moms how they have solved some of these issues in their homes. Perhaps one of their solutions will be yours as well.

Here is a situation we faced in our home. Winter hats and gloves were driving us crazy. Have you ever searched through a box with nine other family member's hats and gloves to find your own? If each of us had two sets of gloves and two hats, that meant there were sixty items in that box to dig through. We struggled with this for several winters. Finally, one year, Steve said he could make "cubbies" for the younger children to put their hats and mittens in. It would be similar to what you see in school and each child would have one.

Steve made the "cubbies" and mounted them low on the inside of the coat closet wall. It was the beginning of the solution. As the children grew, so did their hats and mittens, which then began falling out of the cubbies.

The next solution came in the form of an old dresser. It had ten drawers in it—one for each of us. We have an enclosed front porch so there was space on the porch for the new "hat and glove" dresser. There is room in each drawer for more than one set of those winter items, plus scarves and other miscellaneous winter wear.

Organizational issues are solvable. There is no reason for them to steal our meek and quiet spirits. In fact, it is sad that we would allow them to be so monumental in our lives rather than praying for solutions and waiting for those solutions to come. Our families are much more precious to us than some clutter here or a pile of laundry there.

Which organizational issues are coming between you and a meek and quiet spirit? Why not pray about solutions to them? Addressing these issues can set aside the frustration they cause. In addition, you will gain the ease of living without the inconveniences these problems bring with them. May we purpose not to be complacent in our homes, letting the organizational challenges overwhelm us. Rather let us face them, with the Lord's help, and overcome them.

Application Projects

1. Schedule a half-hour to an hour a day for organization projects.

2. List the organizational areas that are taking away your meek and quiet spirit. Begin praying about them and working on them during your scheduled time.

3. Consult your husband for organizational issues you can't figure out.

4. Make a list of the master lists you think would be useful. Begin to develop these lists.

5. Start a list of organizational tools you believe would be helpful in your home. Buy them as your budget permits.

Chapter Five

Anger

Nothing is quite so discouraging to the homeschooling mom, who desires to teach with a meek and quiet spirit, as when she finds herself becoming angry over situations in her home. James 1:20 says, "For the wrath of man worketh not the righteousness of God." I think we can easily see the truth of this Scripture. It applies to our home teaching as well. We can undo hours of positive training in seconds when our anger is unleashed.

I have observed a great hunger in homeschooling moms to overcome anger in their lives. We despise our anger, desiring instead to have responses that are filled with the fruit of the Spirit, "But the fruit of the Spirit is love, joy, peace, long-suffering, gentleness, goodness, faith, meekness, temperance . . ." (Galatians 5:22, 23). There are some practical steps we can take as we continually ask the Lord to remove anger from our hearts and to replace it with His fruit.

High Goals, Low Expectations

I can almost be assured that if I become angry with a child, it is because my expectations match my goals for him.

It is essential that we have high, godly goals for our children. We want to lead them to the best of their ability spiritually and educationally. However, in this process of moving toward the goals, we must keep our expectations lower than those goals. When I expect my child to have reached a high goal, then I am likely to become angry with him if he hasn't. On the other hand, if I expect my child to have not yet reached the goal, then my spirit is at peace with the training and teaching process as we strive to reach those goals.

It is so much a matter of perspective. The Lord has given us a definite role in our children's lives. If they are spiritually and educationally mature as children, then why are we to train them up? Why are we told to discipline them? It is because children will spend their childhoods working toward the "high goals" the Lord has set for them. They will make progress toward those goals, but it may not be as quick or discernable as we would like it to be. Aren't we glad the Lord doesn't get angry with us every time we fall short of His goals for us?

Consider for a moment a sin or habit you have that you have been praying about and would like to see changed. Here is a simple example from my life. A few years ago, Steve said he would like me to put a cookie sheet under the electric fry pan so the heat from the fry pan wouldn't damage the kitchen counter. High goal for Mom, but shouldn't be too tough, since she likes to please her husband and surely doesn't want to burn her countertop. However, Mom has NEVER put the cookie sheet under the fry pan in all her life! She is usually preoccupied when working in the kitchen and finds herself forgetting, time after time, to put that cookie sheet in place. I did not want to forget. I did not purpose to ignore my husband's request. I just didn't think about it!

I wonder if sometimes this is true for our children. More often than not, they don't deliberately choose not to do what we have told them in the past. It just doesn't occur to them at the moment; they are still children. If my expectation is that they probably will forget and I will need to remind them, then it is okay. I am expecting to do my "job." However, if I have expected them to remember and they don't, I will be angry with them.

I have trained my children to make their beds in the morning, get dressed, and straighten up their rooms. That is my goal for them. However, my expectation is that they might not have done some or all of these jobs. My husband and I have set consequences for the various parts that might have been neglected. This frees me from anger. I can inspect their morning work and not be angry if the goal wasn't met. I am prepared to deal with it. I am also delighted to praise a good job.

Our Responsibility – Consistent Discipline

Another area of anger that needs to be dealt with is our whole mindset toward issues with our children that require training and discipline. Anger creeps into these situations when I am more concerned about my inconveniences and difficulties than I am about my child's long-term character growth. Otherwise, each time there was a problem, I would be happy for the opportunity to work on the character issues that the Lord is bringing out in this child.

I may have a child who is assigned to take out the trash but frequently forgets. If I speak to him in an irritated tone of voice, it is because I am tired of his forgetfulness and am inconvenienced by it. On the other hand, I can tell myself that part of my job as his mother is to help him learn to be responsible. This gives me a positive purpose in the reminding or giving of a consequence, as the case may be.

Our thoughts and attitudes toward our children's behavior are very important. However, Scripture not only directs us in proper thinking about the situations, but it also gives us clear direction on how to work with those situations. Proverbs 29:17, "Correct thy son, and he shall give thee rest; yea, he shall give delight unto thy soul." A mom who is angry with her child is not at rest and does not have delight unto her soul. Therefore, I see some practical issues to be put into effect concerning consistent correction if we want to be daily living out a meek and quiet spirit. Our consistency in training and correcting our children is critical to a meek and quiet spirit. When we correct consistently, we won't be so easily angered.

We purchased a chore tracking system to help give our children accountability for their chores. It was also to assist me in knowing who was doing what chore and when they did it. Each evening I would go to our chore system, count up the children's colored accountability discs, and put up new chore discs for the next day. It took me several weeks to learn the discipline of adding this job to my normal routine. Would you believe that two years later my children had not become consistent, on their part, to put up an accountability disc on each job disc to indicate it had been completed?

You have no idea the number of times my meek and quiet spirit deserted me during those two years over that chore system. I loved the chore board, because it was so easy to see what the children had done and what they hadn't done. I also despised it, because I couldn't get the children to put up their discs. They were so poor at this task I didn't want to discipline them for their failures, because I felt they would be punished continuously. Why had we failed in accomplishing a simple task? It was because I had no consistent consequence that I was willing to enforce.

Finally, one day I discussed the problem with our children. I asked them to suggest what the discipline should be for not putting a disc on the chore board. Their suggestion was to sit on a chair for fifteen minutes for each disc that wasn't put on. The reasoning was that it was much easier to spend a few seconds putting your disc up than to sit on a chair for fifteen minutes. I decided we would try that.

After we figured out this consistent consequence and I steeled myself to the children living on the chair, the situation began to change. They didn't sit on the chair all day! Once, a couple of them had an hour of chair time from the previous day's failure. However, the next evening all of their discs were up! Another day they might forget a tad bit, but after fifteen minutes on the chair, they were again remembering. Wow! What a simple solution–so obvious–and yet I had allowed this situation to continue for two years, finding it regularly grabbed my meek and quiet spirit! (Because of our family's ongoing struggles finding a practical, workable chore system, in 2006 we published our own chore book and chore system, *Managers of Their Chores*. For more information, please see pages 122-123.)

Consider the example of my son who forgets to take out the trash. First, my expectation needs to be low so I accept the fact that he may forget. Then, I must be happy for the opportunity to continue to teach him responsibility and diligence, qualities he will need when he is supporting a family. Finally, there should be correction that occurs. Maybe this correction will be verbal when he is beginning to develop the habit of emptying the trash. With time, however, he will reach a place where it is obvious he should be remembering rather than forgetting. At this point, consequences must be decided upon and consistently used.

Predetermined Consequences

As we think about the idea of correcting our children, we find ourselves face to face with another area that can deprive us of a meek and quiet spirit. What happens when a child has done something wrong, but you just don't know how to correct for it? Often a mom will become angry at that point, feeling a great deal of frustration and impotence.

Here is how this worked in our home. Sometimes I simply didn't know what the consequence should be for a wrong behavior of a child. I knew the child should have some kind of discipline, but what was appropriate for the particular offense? One day I would give a consequence, the next day no consequence, and the following day I tried a different consequence for the same offense. I expected a discipline to be effective the first time I used it. I found myself feeling continually angry in my child-discipline situations. This was stemming from trying to decide what consequence to use on a spur-of-the-moment basis and from no consistency in my disciplining so the consequences weren't working at all.

Let me explain another scenario that occurred regularly in our home. A child would misbehave, and he needed a consequence. When I was having a bad day, I said to the child, "If you do that again, this will be your discipline." It was a huge consequence because I was emotionally unhappy. Several days later, the child did the same thing. It was one of my good days, and I had completely forgotten the promised discipline. However, all of my other children remembered and reminded me. At that point, I realized it was too great a consequence for the offense. I was stuck, though, and usually felt angry with the predicament.

Determining ahead of time what the discipline would be for the normal problems that arose among our children, freed me from the anger I had regularly experienced when consequences were required for the children. This sounds quite simple, and it truly is. Having these decisions made ahead of time meant there was no guesswork. There was no irritation over not knowing what to do. The consequence didn't depend upon my mood. I didn't need to be angry about having to correct the child. It was all lined out for me.

If you need help in this area, I suggest an "If/Then Chart."[1] This chart is an outline containing common children's offenses with the consequence column left blank. The parents determine consequences that they believe are appropriate for their children and write them in the blank column. The chart is mounted on the wall. When there is a problem involving your child, you go to the chart where you can read to the child what he did, the Scripture that applies, and the correction.

We have prayerfully worked to determine effective and practical consequences for our children. Let me share a couple with you to stimulate your thinking for what would be useful to you. Proverbs 17:1 says, "Better *is* a dry morsel, and quietness therewith, than a house full of sacrifices *with* strife." In our home, squabbling between the younger children is not without consequences. Since no one in the family particularly cares to eat the heels of our homemade bread, we use them as an object lesson with built-in correction. When two children are filled with strife toward each other, we tell them that they are to eat a dry crust. We set our crusts out to "cure" thoroughly for several days so they are available for these situations. We repeat Proverbs 17:1, explaining to them how valuable peace and quietness is compared to strife.

Another consequence we have instituted comes from Proverbs 30:32, "If thou hast done foolishly in lifting up thyself, or if thou hast thought evil, *lay* thine hand upon thy mouth." Isn't it the small things, like a child's constant interrupting, that will eventually build up to a point where the meek and quiet spirit is lost? In this case, we literally have the child, who is interrupting, place his hand over his mouth and hold it there for a few minutes. We call this our "hand-over-the-mouth" consequence. Rather than ignoring interrupting, or telling the child over and over to wait patiently, and then finally "yelling" at him, it is better to begin giving a gentle consequence that we won't mind enforcing.

Sweetness of the Lips

Let's consider another practical way to avoid anger stealing our meek and quiet spirit. Proverbs 16:21 teaches us, "The wise in heart shall be called prudent: and the sweetness of the lips increaseth learning." I encourage you to memorize this verse! Use "sweetness of the lips" in all your teaching interactions with your children, which will include not only homeschooling but many discipline situations as well.

Proverbs 15:1 says, "A soft answer turneth away wrath: but grievous words stir up anger." When we don't give "soft answers" to our children, but rather use "grievous words," we are likely to cause them to respond angrily to us. Then what happens? Their anger can, in turn, spur us to an angry answer that wouldn't normally be our response. I have seen this in my life and became convinced of the truth of Proverbs 22:24, "Make no friendship with an angry man; and with a furious man thou shalt not go." Anger breeds anger. We must choose not to be angry and not let ourselves react to a child's anger.

What does our anger do to our children? Will it cause them to want to speak back angrily as well? Proverbs 29:22 says, "An angry man stirreth up strife, and a furious man aboundeth in transgression." Do you think our anger helps or hinders the Holy Spirit in our children's lives? I would propose that most certainly our anger hinders the Holy Spirit and feeds the fleshly reactions of our children.

As hard as it is to admit, anger is a choice. Are you as easily angered at church as you are at home? Have there been times you were angry with a child, but when the phone rang, you answered in a normal tone of voice? These are real-life demonstrations that we can choose not to be angry but rather have "sweetness of the lips" when we are motivated to do so.

Mommy Policeman

Once, Steve painted a word picture for me that I have recalled regularly. Think about a policeman. His job is to enforce the "laws of the land." When a motorist breaks one of those laws, the policeman pulls that motorist over and writes him a ticket. The policeman calmly, and often with a pleasant smile, tells the motorist what the infraction was and what the penalty will be. The policeman isn't irritated because he has had to pull the same motorist over three times already that day. He doesn't become angry with the motorist for trying to talk him out of the ticket. And, most of all, he certainly doesn't cry!!!

My role in our home is very similar to that policeman. I am to enforce the "laws of the family." My children must be stopped frequently and given a ticket. What is my attitude going to be? Will I matter-of-factly, with a pleasant look, write my child his ticket and give it to him (in a manner of speaking)? Will I be frustrated by the constancy of my job and by the fact that I have already given the same child a similar ticket? Will I become angry over it? Will I cry? Will I have a meek and quiet spirit? Sometimes having the proper picture of our role, along with lowering those expectations, is essential to a meek and quiet spirit. It all works together!

Strong and Courageous

As we are striving toward consistency in disciplining our children so that they will give us rest and bring delight to our souls, we need to be strong and courageous (Joshua 1:7). Our "mothers' hearts" can work against us. We want to shelter our children from the very consequences we have agreed, with our husbands, will be for the child's best interest. It may go like this, "Mary, if you don't finish that math lesson, you know you will have to spend your free time, this afternoon, doing it. Everyone else will be outside having fun while you are in here. You don't want that to happen, do you?" Not once, but several times through the school day, you may find yourself continuing to remind Mary to keep at her task. Each time you do this reminding, you may also discover that you don't have as meek and quiet a spirit as you did the time before.

Prodding the children, even with the intention of helping them avoid consequences, can be a meek and quiet spirit snatcher as well. We grow tired of cajoling and not seeing results. Before long, we find ourselves "nagging" in an irritated tone rather than continuing with the pleasant nudging we began. Of course, there will be times mercy is appropriate. It may also be that the training of a child consists of Mom reminding, for a season, until self-control is developed in that child. When this is not the case, though, be strong and courageous; allow the consequences to do their work!

I loathe the consequences my children sometimes choose because of their behavior! Our child who is the biggest dawdler is also the one who seems to most need and crave his free time. My mother heart wants that time for him! However, as my husband and I have prayed and talked about this child, we have agreed that his dawdling will only grow worse if we ignore it. Much more effective than my constant reminding him to stay on task with his schoolwork is his loss of play privileges when he hasn't completed his assignments! He learns the valuable lessons of diligence and responsibility, and I have a meek and quiet spirit.

Proactive

There is still more we can do to avoid the anger that will seize our meek and quiet spirit. Have you ever considered how much of your day is spent on the defensive when dealing with almost insignificant discipline issues such as: flush the toilet, don't slam the door, chew with your mouth closed, hang up your coat? Often these little situations are the ones that build up to the point where anger bursts from continual frustration.

What about being on the offensive? A pastor of ours used to say, "Nothing becomes dynamic until it becomes specific." Do you want your children to put their shoes and socks away when they take them off? Then you will need to have a time set aside in your day when you are training them to do this task. During training time, you can talk with them about the rewards of orderliness and what a blessing it will be to them and to their family. You can go through a math problem illustrating how many shoes and socks will be out in the house if every member, daily, leaves two pairs of each out. The children can practice taking off their shoes and socks, and putting them away, over and over, during your training time.

Work on a handful of tasks and attitudes during training time until you are comfortable that the children are beginning to implement them during the day on their own. Then you can move on to new areas while continuing to reinforce, through the day, what they have already learned during training. Training sessions are offensive and proactive!

In addition, I would encourage you to tie Scripture to what you are training your children in. Let them see a purpose in God's Word for what they are doing. If you know any songs to reinforce the teaching, use them, or make some up to be sung as the task is being done. My children love to write their own little booklets to illustrate what they are learning. Then they read these books frequently, which reinforces what I have been teaching them.

The possibilities for proactive teaching and training are endless. Every task you thoroughly train your children to do will reduce the number of things that may cause you to lose your meek and quiet spirit. Here are a few more possible subjects for proactive training time: morning rising routine, proper hand washing, clothes folding, first time obedience, and sweet conversation between siblings.

Remember, the lessons learned during training time need to be put into practice throughout the day. The more you praise and encourage each time you see a child doing what he has been taught, the more you will see that behavior blossom. Almost all children inherently desire to please their parents. Praise goes far in promoting the learning that you want. "Pleasant words *are as* a honeycomb, sweet to the soul, and health to the bones" (Proverbs 16:24).

Those We Love the Most

Sadly, anger is no stranger among homeschooling moms. I can remember, as a little girl, that my parents would frequently ask my sister and me, "Why do we treat a stranger more kindly than we do our own family members?" This is so true. While we would never allow ourselves to outwardly display anger toward someone in a public setting, we will excuse ourselves to be angry with our own family–the ones we love the very most!

If we choose not to be angry when we are in public, is it not possible we can do the same within our home? Obviously if we can't, our fear of man is mistakenly greater than our fear of God. Proverbs 16:6 says, "By mercy and truth iniquity is purged: and by the fear of the LORD *men* depart from evil." (See also *Anger–Relationship Poison* audio, www.Titus2.com.)

We will quickly undermine most of the good we are trying to accomplish in our homeschooling if we allow anger to steal our meek and quiet spirit. Children are very quick to ignore anything we say to them when we are angry. They can even become fearful and mistrusting of us, not able to judge what will and what won't set us off.

Truly, our heart's desire must be, as completely as possible, to rid ourselves of all anger. Remember these words each time anger threatens your meek and quiet spirit: *"It is better to dwell in the wilderness, than with a contentious and an angry woman"* (Proverbs 21:19).

Recall again with me James 1:20. "For the wrath of man worketh not the righteousness of God." Let us never, never, never excuse our anger! Rather, after confession and repentance, may we seek the Lord for practical ways to avoid anger when possible and then to deal with it when necessary. Let us humbly keep our hearts lifted in prayer to the Lord for His victory, that the fruit of the Spirit would be manifest in our lives through a meek and quiet spirit.

Application Projects

1. Pray about and list your goals for each child. Evaluate your expectations in light of your goals.

2. Determine consequences for the discipline issues you face with your children. Write these consequences down and use them!

3. Listen to yourself as you interact with your children. Do you speak angrily to them, or are you pleasant with them?

4. Set up a training time, particularly for younger children, when you will teach them what they need to know for their daily tasks.

---

1. We carry the "If/Then Chart" on our website, www.Titus2.com, or you may call, (913) 772-0392.

Chapter Six

Hard Work and Dying to Self

Perhaps these meek and quiet spirit robbers should be our wake-up call to the fact that homeschooling and home-making require hard work. They are demanding and time consuming. We are called to put forth effort and to push ourselves day after day after day. There are no "free rides." If we kick back for a day, or two, or three and ignore it all, it will still be waiting for us and more!

I encourage all of us, as homeschooling moms, to see the work level required in our task as a holy calling from the Lord, no different from Paul's race. 1 Corinthians 9:24-27, "Know ye not that they which run in a race run all, but one receiveth the prize? So run, that ye may obtain. And every man that striveth for the mastery is temperate in all things. Now they do it to obtain a corruptible crown; but we an incorruptible. I therefore so run, not as uncertainly; so fight I, not as one that beateth the air: But I keep under my body, and bring it into subjection: lest that by any means, when I have preached to others, I myself should be a castaway."

Recall some of the most godly Christian men and women you have known, read about, and heard of. What were their days like? Did they completely spend themselves in serving the Lord? Of course! In a like manner, we are called to do the same. We may never have a book written about us or be remembered by the world, but our children will bear the results in their lives, as well as future generations of our family, because we were willing to work hard. Proverbs 31:28 reminds us, "Her children arise up, and call her blessed . . ."

Time to Myself?

I remember speaking to a lovely young mother after giving a workshop at a homeschooling conference. She had four children, ages six and under. She came up wondering how she could get more time in her day to herself. I suggested she rise early enough in the morning so she would have time alone with the Lord before the children were awake. I also encouraged her to have an hour or more each afternoon when all the children napped or did quiet activities. That would be another hour of quiet time for her to use as the Lord directed. This mom assured me she already had those times worked into her schedule, but she needed more time to herself.

The responsibilities of being a mother and of homeschooling do not allow us to have great quantities of time to ourselves. Little children require our constant supervision. I have been very happy to have early morning and afternoon nap time reprieves from the activity level of my young children. As a matter of fact, the Lord has had to work with me because having a child interrupt one of these times, which I considered "my time" each day, was likely to claim my meek and quiet spirit rather quickly.

Our Mentors

Many homeschooling moms were raised in homes where their mothers were home all day while the children went away to school. If our moms wanted to, they had six or more hours a day to devote to housecleaning, laundry, and organizing. Perhaps because they stayed home, having time to do lots of housework, they were of the "children are only children once" philosophy. This often meant they didn't require very much of us as far as chores and responsibilities were concerned.

From this kind of upbringing, we find several factors that could work against us. First, we may compare our homes to what we remember our mothers' homes were like. While it certainly is possible to keep a neat and tidy home while homeschooling, it won't be the same standard of cleanliness that it would if we spent four hours a day on it. Moreover, there is a greater opportunity for mess and clutter to accumulate when the children are home all day, rather than away at school for seven hours.

The second difficulty we may encounter is that we didn't learn the housekeeping tasks that we so desperately need. Our mothers did many of these jobs when we were at school. We didn't learn by observation because we weren't around. If a mom didn't make a pointed effort to teach her daughter these skills, then the girl has had to develop them as need arose in her own home.

Perhaps you came from a home where your mom did work outside the home. Somehow, though, she managed to keep up with her meals, laundry, housework, family, and outside work. However, she didn't teach you her homemaking skills, because she generally didn't have the time. You, as well, may be comparing yourself to a standard you saw your mother set. These kinds of comparisons squelch a meek and quiet spirit!

I was interested when one day on MOTHBoard (www.Titus2.com) a mom wrote to say she had noticed, in reading *Managers of Their Homes*, I damp mopped my vinyl floors only once a month. She had to do hers at least once a day. I couldn't imagine doing mine once a day! I tried to remember how often my mom mopped her floors. I really didn't know. I wasn't home when she mopped the floors, and as a child, I sure didn't notice, when I came home, what she had done or not done that day!

I realized I had figured out how often to mop my kitchen floor based on what I deemed to be its need. We vacuumed that floor three times a week. However, the reason I didn't mop it very often was that it was quite old, had no shine left on it, and a pattern that didn't show much. When we put light colored vinyl in our bathroom, it was a different story. That floor needs daily sweeping and weekly mopping.

Another comparison we may bring from our childhood is that of a mom who could spend her evenings and weekends relaxing with the family. When I was growing up, it was common for a family to spend several hours each night watching television after dinner. Since the mom had spent the day doing her homemaking tasks, she was free to enjoy this time with her husband and children.

As homeschooling moms, we find that we must keep going through the evening and weekend hours to accomplish tasks such as laundry, cleaning, correspondence, and organizational issues. We may not be able to sit back and "relax" every evening.

We spend several hours of each day homeschooling. Is it too great a sacrifice for us to continue to work through hours that might otherwise be considered "free" time? Are we willing to give of ourselves, in selfless investment, in the eternal futures of our children? John 12:24-25 says, "Verily, verily, I say unto you, Except a corn of wheat fall into the ground and die, it abideth alone: but if it die, it bringeth forth much fruit. He that loveth his life shall lose it; and he that hateth his life in this world shall keep it unto life eternal." Perhaps some of that fruit will be our own meek and quiet spirit. Perhaps some will be fruit in our children's lives.

"And he said to them all, If any man will come after me, let him deny himself, and take up his cross daily, and follow me" (Luke 9:23). Following the Lord through home-schooling will cause us to daily deny ourselves and take up our cross. It is imperative that we keep the truth of God's Word in our minds and hearts so we don't become resentful toward our workload.

Rather, it is our desire, as the woman in Proverbs 31:27 demonstrates, to "looketh well to the ways of her household, and eateth not the bread of idleness." Consider the results the woman experiences from this: "Her children arise up, and call her blessed; her husband also, and he praiseth her" (Proverbs 31:28).

Your Husband's Free Time

I wonder how this scenario causes you to feel. You have been busy all day homeschooling, getting some laundry done, had an hour of cleaning, made all the meals, and now dinner is over. Your husband heads for his easy chair in the living room and kicks back with the newspaper, while you head to the kitchen to clean up after dinner.

Years ago, if this would happen at our house, it could cause me to "stew" all evening! I wasn't close to having a meek and quiet spirit. Through the subsequent years, the Lord began to teach me valuable lessons about being a help meet to my husband. Genesis 2:18 says, "And the Lord God said, It is not good that the man should be alone; I will make him a help meet for him."

As our family grew, I had come to see Steve as my help meet. I wanted him to help with dinner cleanup in the evenings. I thought he should watch over the children while he was home. If he gave the children their baths some nights, I felt that was only fair. Certainly, his help putting the children to bed seemed like a necessity to me.

The Lord had to bring me to Genesis 2:18, repeatedly, as He gently led me in learning my role as a wife. I was the help meet. Steve was not my help meet.

Steve often lightens my load during the evening hours. He loves to spend those hours with the children. Many years ago, he took over the weekly grocery shopping so I could have an hour at home to myself with the "command" from him to take a bath. He puts the three little boys to bed each evening. However, his doing these tasks did not come because of my complaining to him or nagging him to do them. Rather, they were an extension of his love for me and a physical way of demonstrating it.

Viewing myself as a help meet was greatly beneficial to my meek and quiet spirit. I was able to serve joyfully, even if Steve wasn't working beside me. I no longer entertained expectations of what he should be doing when he was home with the children and me. In addition, it allowed me to be grateful for everything Steve did that I considered helpful in my realm.

Titus 2

"The aged likewise ... that they may teach the young women to be sober, to love their husbands, to love their children, to be discreet, chaste, keepers at home, good, obedient to their own husbands, that the word of God be not blasphemed" (Titus 2:3-5). As I read this list of what the older women are to teach the younger women, I don't find much that leads me to believe there is to be lots of "down" time. Don't misunderstand me. I am not saying we should never sit for a few minutes, relax, or simply do nothing. Rather, I am encouraging us to accept the fullness of our homeschooling lifestyle with joy instead of resentment. When we have the realistic expectation that our days will be very busy and that there will be much hard work, then we will be more likely to maintain a meek and quiet spirit. If we think we'll have our evenings and weekends free, then we will be frustrated and angry when we can't fit our homeschooling, plus our other homemaking tasks, into just the weekdays.

There was a time in my homeschooling career when this was my goal–to have those evenings and weekends free. That goal came with a high price tag. There was no time for preschool with my littlest children, reading out loud to the children, having individual time with a child, or sewing matching outfits for the girls. My free time centered on what I thought my needs were.

How much happier my heart was and how much more content I became in my role as a homeschooling mother when I gave up trying to have evenings and weekends free. Putting those special times with my children into my day was so much better than being free in the evenings. You probably won't be surprised to know that I do still have some free time. I enjoy it when it is there, but it isn't a "demand" in my life any more.

May I encourage you, as well, to be willing to be like a grain of wheat, falling to the ground and dying so that you may bring forth fruit. Can you take up your cross daily as you follow Christ? What a wonderful way to walk with a meek and quiet spirit when our eyes are off of ourselves. We must keep our focus on the Lord and on obediently serving our family, knowing it involves hard work!

Application Projects

1. Make a list of the times you would like to have for yourself. Are the items on this list realistic? Are they reasonable? Are they part of "dying to self"?

2. Make a list of how you think your husband should help you. Commit this list to the Lord through prayer, and commit yourself to learning to be a help meet to your husband.

3. Spend some time considering whether you are trying to pattern your free time after your mother's. Evaluate how your life is different from hers, and what impact that has on what you can accomplish.

Chapter Seven

Depression

In one of Steve's monthly homeschooling articles for dads (www.Titus2.com; July 2000), he mentioned that my bouts with depression were part of the reason we decided, at one point, to limit our family size. We were amazed at how many people e-mailed us, after that one sentence in his article, to ask how we had dealt with the problem of depression. It seemed fitting to put together our thoughts on a subject we would be just as happy to shove into the closet and forget was ever a part of our lives. However, there is the possibility that our experience and the changes the Lord has brought in this area might be helpful to others.[1] Certainly, depression plays a huge role in the stealing of a meek and quiet spirit.

It has only been the eight years since the Lord has given me freedom from the at-times-devastating depression with which I had struggled. It was usually worst during the year I nursed a baby. My pain through those difficult years was very real and is not that distant. I can fully understand the concerned feelings of a mom who is struggling with times of depression, and the worry of her husband, because that was our experience too.

I can't point to a miracle cure, nor did I discover a twelve-step program to overcome depression. This is probably so I can take no pride in what I did but always know it was the Lord's work. I will share what we see, in retrospect, about things that helped move me away from depression, and perhaps there will be something here that the Lord can use in another's life.

The Lord's Timing

One of my first lessons to learn was that the Lord works in His time. I wanted to be over the emotional downs right away. I didn't want it to be "in process," and sometimes I was even angry with God because He wasn't helping me to be better right away. If He was the One to work in my life and I was still depressed, angry, and struggling, then it was His fault! That thinking was totally wrong, but that was how far off my ability to think truth had moved. I had to learn to accept my failings and sinfulness and wait on the Lord for what He would do in my life. It was not my timetable. Philippians 2:13, "For it is God which worketh in you both to will and to do of his good pleasure."

My depression was humbling because I knew I wasn't what I should be or what He wanted me to be. I even confessed to my church family what was going on in my life. That was a start towards the healing process for me. The depression was no longer something I had hidden away in my private life. Rather, now the Lord could use the prayers of my church family to help me.

I stayed faithful to daily Bible reading and prayed through those dark times, even though I might feel distant from and forgotten by the Lord. However, in the midst of those black days, I was sometimes closer to the Lord than I have ever been. This was because I was totally helpless and needy, not knowing where to turn or what to do.

Physical Factors

We discovered that there were very real hormonal imbalances that affected my emotions. I would do everything I could to deny this, but it was obvious to everyone except me. What I could normally handle one day would send me into tears another day. To combat this physical imbalance, I used the natural progesterone cream for a time.[2] In addition, I followed a vitamin regime suggested by our naturopathic doctor friend.[3] I eliminated caffeine as well.

Daily exercise was critical at this time. I know daily exercise sounds impossible to an already depressed, over-whelmed, terribly tired mom. My walks were about the only time I was away from home. When I began to feel myself spiraling down, getting out would sometimes be the single thing that would change the course of my emotions. Just being away from the environment I was struggling with for a short period each day, plus the effect of the exercise itself, was very helpful.

Being tired was sure to put me off balance. I am a light sleeper, often being awakened in the night by a noise or perhaps the need to nurse a baby. After that, I wouldn't be able to go back to sleep. For eight years now, I have worn earplugs when I sleep.[4] They have transformed my nights! I thought not being able to sleep was just a part of my physical makeup. Not so! Since I began wearing earplugs, I hardly ever have a sleepless night. Steve became the "ears" for our family. I know he will wake me up if the children need me. (Earplugs may not be an option for a mom whose husband can't do this.)

If you want to see what being tired does to even the most "spiritual" of people, look at Scripture. The story of Elijah running from Jezebel after the Mt. Carmel experience is a great example. Elijah was tired, and 1 Kings 19:3-5 tells us what happened: "And when he saw that, he arose, and went for his life, and came to Beersheba, which belongeth to Judah, and left his servant there. But he himself went a day's journey into the wilderness, and came and sat down under a juniper tree: and he requested for himself that he might die; and said, It is enough; now, O Lord, take away my life; for I am not better than my fathers. And as he lay and slept under a juniper tree, behold, then an angel touched him, and said unto him, Arise and eat."

Sisters, guard sufficient sleep in your life very carefully. Don't trade it for quiet, late nights when the children are asleep, and you can have some peace. It isn't worth it!

Acceptance, Not Analysis

I discovered I made it best through a time of depression when I didn't try to analyze what was causing it. It was better to accept my feelings–as Steve would encourage me to do–like a physical ailment to be patiently waited out. The more I ferreted for the causes, the more discouraged and upset I would become.

However, the times I accepted the feelings and said, "Lord, I don't like this, but I'm going to focus on You and not on me. I am not going to make any major decisions or search for the cause. I will just wait. If I do that, it will pass with no damage except for feeling down. If I think about being depressed, and talk to Steve about it, it will pull me further down, resulting in wrong thoughts and words."

When Steve had run out of ideas for how to help me on his own, he found a pastor's wife who agreed to counsel with me. Janice and I met in person one time for an afternoon. She started by making sure that I knew I was saved (see Chapter 2). With that assurance, she then gave me a couple of tangible projects to put my focus on the Lord rather than on myself. I called her a few times on the phone–at Steve's insistence–and the path she set me on was exactly what I needed.

Here are two of her projects. Perhaps they will be helpful to you as well. The first project involved learning to take captive my wrong thoughts–thoughts of being depressed, thoughts that I was going to ruin my children, thoughts that I would never feel normal, thoughts of anger, bitterness, or defeat, and thoughts of being overwhelmed. Those thoughts were all lies! 2 Corinthians 10:5 is now one of my favorite verses. It says, "Casting down imaginations, and every high thing that exalteth itself against the knowledge of God, and bringing into captivity every thought to the obedience of Christ." I was to take my thoughts captive to the obedience of Christ! For example, the truth concerning the feeling of being overwhelmed is that the Lord hasn't given me one more thing than there is time to do. If there isn't time to do it, then He doesn't expect it of me. My family was better off with next to nothing being done than with my trying to do everything my expectations said needed to be done while I was depressed, with my mind running in circles and unable to concentrate.

The pastor's wife encouraged me to begin a notebook. She showed me hers. It was a simple 8½-by-11-inch three-ring binder with "ABC" tabs in it. Behind the tabs she had notebook paper, each with a topic on it, such as "Anger," "Discouragement," "Discipline," etc. When she had her Bible reading time, she would take verses that applied to her and copy them down in her notebook under an appropriate heading. Then, when she needed to think "truth," she could open her notebook and read it.

I would suggest that moms who are prone to depression do this kind of evaluation of what you are thinking and replace any lies with God's truth. Begin a notebook such as I have described. If you can't think of God's truth–I know there were many times when I couldn't–get your Bible or notebook out and find that truth. Speak it aloud if necessary! Sometimes, I would have to say words of truth aloud because my thinking was so muddled and twisted. I could not concentrate on or accept the truth when it remained only in my mind. However, when I spoke the words, my heart would grab hold of them!

For the second project, I was to have another section of the notebook titled "Sin List." Every time I sinned, I was to write it in the notebook. I was then to confess the sin to the Lord, repent of it, and ask His forgiveness. In my notebook, I would write "FORGIVEN" over that sin. This helped me to let go of my failures rather than letting them overwhelm me.

No Condemnation

How do you handle it when you are depressed? Do you become increasingly unhappy with yourself for being depressed, making the downward cycle even worse? I would do that, or I would end up becoming angry with the children and "beat" myself up about that. In my Mom's Corner from February 2000, called "No Condemnation" (www.Titus2.com), I share how the Lord gave me victory over that cycle, although I write of it in terms of the struggles I have now. However, the truths I apply with my current problems are the ones the Lord taught me in the depths of my need. Learning "no condemnation" came from the "Sin List" project Janice gave me.

I believe a most powerful change came when I made a decision before the Lord one morning. I remember thinking, "Lord, I just feel like crying all the time. I am miserable. My family is miserable. I can't seem to do anything about how I feel, but I can do something about how my family feels. I can act like I am happy whether I feel like it or not. My emotions don't have to drive my behavior, and I can make that choice because of my love for my family." Those reading this who are living with depression may think this would be impossible for you to do. I encourage you to test yourself. When you are down and go to church, can others tell by looking at you and talking to you that you are depressed? If you can make this choice to act differently from how you feel there, you can do it at home!

I think if depression-prone moms could figure out a way to work on even a skeleton of a schedule, it would help. I have had moms write to me that when they are depressed, brain dead, or just overwhelmed, their schedule directed them through the day. This was especially helpful because they couldn't make decisions themselves. If you have somewhat of a schedule in place, despite tiredness or feelings, many things would be accomplished because it is the easiest path to take–just do what the schedule says! Without my schedule on those bad days, I would have simply sat and cried. That would have made everything even worse because then I would have been a day behind! In addition, you can let your schedule direct your children when you don't have the energy to keep up with what you would like to be doing. At least they are accomplishing things rather than just undoing everything.

Hope in the Lord

If it is any encouragement, I asked my older children if they remembered the struggles I had during those early, difficult days of their lives. My two oldest boys, who are now adults, recall nothing negative. Can you believe the Lord might blind our children to what is going on inside of us especially when so much of it is easily visible? My adult daughter only remembers one time I was really struggling. I don't share that as a license to allow hormones or depression to control your life and emotions. Rather, I tell it to help you not feel that it is ever hopeless, even if you think there is too much emotional damage already done to the children and to you.

Twenty-three years ago I would never have believed where the Lord would bring me in relation to depression. I thought it was impossible to be free of it, but I am! The process was gradual. I wanted it to happen right away. Looking back, fifteen years isn't all that long of a wait to lose what was such a devastating, negative part of my life.

As women, God created us such that there are emotions and hormones to be coped with. That is still true in my life. However, a disappointment, a "down" day, a discouraging situation is nothing more than that. These no longer send me spiraling through depression. They are simply normal burdens to be left with my Lord Jesus while I rest in Him.

I pray the Lord will give each mom who needs help in the area of depression insight into what will make a difference. Steve always encouraged me that as long as my heart's desire was to please the Lord, He would answer that heart's cry.

Somehow, these words don't come close to describing what those years were like. My prayer is that you will sense in my heart a deep desire to be able to encourage moms that it can be better. This is true even if you are homeschooling, if there are more pregnancies and babies, or if there are more challenges of any kind. My growing out of the depressions was a result, I believe, of a process the Lord brought me through in the midst of homeschooling, pregnancies, and babies. Seek the Lord!

Application Projects

1. Rest in the Lord.

2. Pray.

3. Make a notebook.

4. List your failures and ask God to forgive you.

5. Begin writing truth.

6. Act happy even if you don't feel like it.

Notes:

1. I am not a doctor; I cannot make medical recommendations. I am only sharing my own personal experiences. I encourage each of you to pray and research as you look for your solutions to depression.

2. Natural progesterone cream can be found in most health food stores. The progesterone cream I used is called ProGest and can be purchased from Transitions for Health, Inc. Emerita. 1-800-888-6814 or www.transitionsforhealth.com.

3. You would need to research the vitamins on your own, because I no longer have that list.

4. The ear plugs I use are the soft, spongy type. They are called "Classic" by Cabot Safety Corporation, 317-692-6666.

Chapter Eight

Gratitude, Contentment, and a Smile

Much of what we have been considering so far has dealt with a defensive attitude, trying to avoid what deprives us of that meek and quiet spirit. Now let us move on to what will strengthen a meek and quiet spirit from an offensive point of view, in addition to our time alone with the Lord. There are three areas I want us to look at together. They are gratitude, contentment, and a smile.

Gratitude

"In every thing give thanks: for this is the will of God in Christ Jesus concerning you" (1 Thessalonians 5:18). I would venture to say when we don't have a meek and quiet spirit, we are not giving thanks. The opposite would be true as well. If we are giving thanks, we probably will have a meek and quiet spirit.

Here is one of these very clear verses with great practical application. Haven't we often said, "If I just knew what God's will was, I would do it!" In this case, we do know God's will. It is spelled out very clearly. Yet, I find myself grumbling in my heart about situations, which isn't even close to giving thanks.

For example, I am quite prone to frustration and irritation with my children for not putting their things away. Consider that there can often be ten Maxwell family members home all day every day, since Steve and our older boys have their offices in our basement. If each person leaves out just five items a day, that is three hundred and fifty things lying around the house by the end of the week! Can you imagine?

I could choose to be angry and grumble in my heart as I pick up, as I remind, as I discipline, or as I ignore the mess—whatever the case may be. On the other hand, I could give thanks. To do this I must stop thinking about "poor Teri" and how much work her family makes for her. Instead, I will meditate on my love for my children. I can be grateful that we have these items in our home. I could thank the Lord for the ongoing opportunities to teach my children to be orderly and responsible. There are even times when it is appropriate to be happy for the opportunity to continue to develop a servant's heart by doing others' picking up for them.

It all boils down to what I am thinking about. Am I bringing those thoughts into obedience to Christ (2 Corinthians 10:5)? Am I letting my mind dwell on my own perceived hardships? "Set your affection on things above, not on things on the earth" (Colossians 3:2). The more my thoughts are on the Lord, the more I am able to love my family with a meek and quiet spirit.

When negative emotions come over me, it is usually because I am thinking about myself. I become angry with the children because it is an inconvenience to me to have to correct them or to be patient with them. If I am truly grateful for the opportunity to raise them as soldiers for the Lord, then I will be excited for every chance there is to train them. If I really am grateful to be able to give a cup of cold water in Jesus' name, I won't mind getting up to help a child with a drink.

My children are so happy when I am grateful for them and what they do. They love to be appreciated. They delight when I notice what they do and express my gratitude to them. Just today, one of my sons said to me, "Thank you, Mommy, for telling me my sentences were good." It takes such a small amount of gratitude or praise to bring a happy heart to our children. I certainly like it when the tables are reversed, and my children thank me for something.

Contentment

Contentment is another quality that greatly influences whether we will manifest a meek and quiet spirit. It is easy to always want things to be different. We buy the new spelling curriculum that the other homeschoolers are raving about. As we begin to use it, our children complain about how much work it is. It sure doesn't make us content to have a child who is unhappy with his schoolwork. In addition, it may be that we aren't seeing the results we had hoped for from the new spelling materials. Soon we are discontent with what we thought would be the perfect spelling curriculum just as we were discontent with what we had used previously.

There are times when I could allow my thoughts to wander through what I might do with my days if I weren't homeschooling. This only leads to discontentment. Maybe you wonder what it would be like if your husband were more of a spiritual leader in your home. Perhaps you think about how much easier your job would be if your children were more cooperative and had better attitudes. These thoughts and others like them cause discontentment, a real meek and quiet spirit snatcher!

Contentment and gratitude are tightly bound together. If I am grateful that I can stay home with my children and homeschool, then I am going to be content in what I am doing. If I am thankful for each of my children, I will not wish they were different or that they would not bring trials into my life. When I am thinking about my husband's positive traits, I am grateful for him. When I am praising him, I am content with the leadership he provides in our home.

"But godliness with contentment is great gain" (1 Timothy 6:6). "Not that I speak in respect of want: for I have learned, in whatsoever state I am, therewith to be content. I know both how to be abased, and I know how to abound: every where and in all things I am instructed both to be full and to be hungry, both to abound and to suffer need" (Philippians 4:11-12). These are excellent verses to memorize and meditate upon if there is lack of contentment in your life.

A Smile

Have you ever stared at yourself in the mirror thinking, "Wow, I am looking pretty ragged!" Then you smile into that mirror and see an amazing transformation. Try it!

I am a serious person by nature. While smiling at others in public comes easily, when I am about my daily tasks, it doesn't. Quite often, though, I am the one holding the keys to the atmosphere in our home. When I make a concerted effort to smile, everyone in the family seems to put on a smile as well.

A smile conveys love, acceptance, warmth, and understanding. It is almost always appropriate within a family. It might be good for us to have little mirrors on our children's foreheads so that we could see how we look as we are teaching them, disciplining them, playing with them, or just talking with them. Is our countenance pleasant or harsh? Is it interested or bored? Would we see joy or disappointment?

Here is what happens to me. When I smile on the outside, even if I don't feel like it, I am more likely to soon begin to have a smile on the inside as well. It seems to me that an inner smile is a beautiful picture of a meek and quiet spirit. A smile characterizes those words that describe a meek and quiet spirit: mild of temper, soft, gentle, not easily provoked or irritated, peaceable, not turbulent, not giving offense, mild, and contented.

As homeschooling moms, keeping our thoughts and attitudes positive by being grateful and content will help us toward meek and quiet spirits. A smile is a contagious outward sign of the meek and quiet spirit within. If that spirit is not present, a forced smile can sometimes transfer its spirit to the inside. While possible, it is truly difficult to genuinely smile on the outside while stewing on the inside.

May we be committed to seeking the Lord for a contented heart if we don't already have one. It is certainly in God's will to learn to be grateful. I pray that we won't say these are qualities that are too elusive for us, too unnatural, or too difficult. Rather, we can choose to truly lift our voices in prayer with an earnest desire for a smile on our faces and contented, grateful hearts.

Application Projects

1. List the things in your family and home you are grateful for. Make an effort to express this gratitude throughout the day.

2. List what you are content with in your life. List what you are not content with in your life. Evaluate what you are not content with. Are they areas the Lord is calling you to grow in spiritually or to work on? How might you be grateful for each of those difficult areas? Are they areas in which you need to learn contentment?

3. Make an effort to smile more!

Chapter Nine

The Power of a Meek and Quiet Spirit

Day in and day out, the Lord gives us opportunities to live out our faith. Often the evidence of this faith is a meek and quiet spirit. How will we react to the trials, difficulties, irritations, stresses, and inconveniences that are a part of every homeschool day? We do not have to be caught in the sinful reactions that have continually been a part of our lives. "And ye shall know the truth, and the truth shall make you free" (John 8:32).

How many of us can say we have learned the realities of James 1:2-4? "My brethren, count it all joy when ye fall into divers temptations; Knowing this, that the trying of your faith worketh patience. But let patience have her perfect work, that ye may be perfect and entire, wanting nothing." What about 2 Corinthians 12:10, "Therefore I take pleasure in infirmities, in reproaches, in necessities, in persecutions, in distresses for Christ's sake: for when I am weak, then am I strong"?

These are strong verses telling us what our reaction to difficulties should be. Do we have a meek and quiet spirit? How will we respond to what is going on around us? Will our thoughts be on our hardships and ourselves? Will we take every thought captive and bring it into the obedience of Christ (2 Corinthians 10:5)? Can we do this in our own strength? Of course not, as 2 Corinthians 12:9 says, "And he said unto me, My grace is sufficient for thee: for my strength is made perfect in weakness. Most gladly therefore will I rather glory in my infirmities, that the power of Christ may rest upon me."

Any struggle for a meek and quiet spirit is an opportunity for the power of Christ to rest upon us. We will face fear, but God has given us a spirit "of power, and of love, and of a sound mind" (2 Timothy 1:7). We probably won't eliminate the fears from coming to us, but we can choose how long they will stay. We can rest on the truth of God's Word in our lives and in our children's lives.

We will certainly have organizational struggles. Will they become the focus of our lives, or will they motivate us to cry out to the Lord for solutions? We can schedule time into our day to work in the areas that need to be de-junked or simply maintained. If they aren't a high enough priority to assign time to, then they shouldn't be meek and quiet spirit robbers.

Anger can rule our lives. We can go from angry encounters, manifested by an irritated tone of voice or a frustrated heart, to an angry outburst. Then after the sin has been committed, we may choose to ignore it and thereby give root to self-pity and worldly sorrow. On the other hand, we can deal with our anger, as Scripture points out we should, by confessing it, repenting of it, and receiving God's grace.

We simply don't have the luxury of excusing any of our anger at all. The consequences are too devastating for us and for our children. Immediate, sincere confession and repentance is the key to victory over anger and the regaining of a meek and quiet spirit.

We can choose to dwell on those difficulties, or we can walk in God's ways knowing He has a purpose for each of them. If our thinking is right, then we can "count it all joy" and "take pleasure in infirmities" because we know that Jesus has a purpose for it.

Do we feel gratitude to the Lord for the privilege He has given us to homeschool, gratitude to our husbands, and gratitude to our children? Gratitude is critical if we are to take our eyes off our troubles and put them on the Giver of every good and perfect gift (James 1:17). Our family and homeschooling are gifts, and too often, we take them for granted or come to view them as curses instead.

Homeschooling is hard work! There is no way around the fact that many hours each day are taken up by homeschooling. This time would be available for other activities if we chose to send our children away to school. Is there a value we can assign to the eternal benefits we expect from homeschooling? We homeschool because the Lord has directed us to do so. Are we willing to give up personal, discretionary time in order to be obedient? When our answer is a joyful "yes," we will have the needed potential to homeschool with a meek and quiet spirit!

Remember, the undergirding of a meek and quiet spirit is your time alone with the Lord. There is no substitution for reading your Bible and becoming intimately acquainted with your Savior. Focused, private prayer is very important as well. Please make sure that nothing continually keeps you from this vital time.

My dear homeschooling sister, teaching with a meek and quiet spirit is a goal well worth investing your time and energies into. You will have a renewed sense of effectiveness in your teaching. Your homeschool will be revitalized. Your children will experience a security in your presence. Even your husband will delight in your meek and quiet spirit!

May we dedicate ourselves to the task of teaching with a meek and quiet spirit. May we pray continually for the Lord's Spirit to work in our hearts to help us overcome meek and quiet spirit robbers. May our hearts be filled with gratitude and contentment. Finally, may we truly homeschool with a meek and quiet spirit!

Additional Resources
by the Maxwells/www.Titus2.com

Managers of Their Homes: A Practical Guide to Daily Scheduling for Christian Homeschool Families, by Steven and Teri Maxwell. Information on page 120.

Managers of Their Chores: A Practical Guide to Children's Chores, by Steven and Teri Maxwell. Information on page 122.

Keeping Our Children's Hearts: Our Vital Priority, by Steven and Teri Maxwell. Information on page 124.

Preparing Sons to Provide for a Single-Income Family, by Steven Maxwell. Information on page 125.

Just Around the Corner: Encouragement and Challenge for Christian Dads and Moms (Vols. 1 and 2) by Steven and Teri Maxwell. Information on page 126.

The Moody Family Series, by Sarah Maxwell. Information on page 127.

Feed My Sheep and *Encouragement for the Homeschool Family* (Audio Resources). Information on page 128.

Managers of Their Homes

A Practical Guide to Daily Scheduling for
Christian Homeschool Families

By Steven and Teri Maxwell

A homeschool mother's greatest challenge may be "getting it all done." *Managers of Their Homes* offers solutions! Responses by families who have read *Managers of Their Homes* and utilized the Scheduling Kit indicate the almost unbelievable improvements they have realized.

Step-by-step instructions and a unique Scheduling Kit make the setting up of a daily schedule easily achievable for any homeschooling family. *"People have told me for years that I need a schedule, but every time I tried I couldn't get one to work. I always had problems fitting everything that needed to be done into one day. With your system, I am actually accomplishing more, and I have more time left over! The key to it is the great worksheets. They are invaluable."* Who wouldn't like to accomplish more and have time left over?

How does one schedule school time? Are you struggling with keeping up in areas such as laundry, dishes, or housekeeping? Does it seem like there is no time for you in the day? Do you feel stressed over the busyness of your days or not accomplishing all you want? It doesn't matter whether you have one child or twelve, this book will help you to plan your daily schedule.

Managers of Their Homes: A Practical Guide to Daily Scheduling for Christian Homeschool Families sets a firm biblical foundation for scheduling, in addition to discussing scheduling's numerous benefits. Chapter after chapter is filled with practical suggestions for efficient, workable ways to schedule a homeschooling family's days. Thirty real-life schedules in the Appendix give valuable insight into creating a personalized schedule. Also included is a special chapter by Steve for homeschool dads.

"My schedule has given me back my sanity!! I can't believe the way my life has changed since implementing a schedule." Tracy L.

"I had read almost every organizational book there was, and I still couldn't get to where I wanted to be until I applied this method!" Corrie

"In retrospect, having used the book, I would have paid $100 for it, if I could have know beforehand the tremendous benefits I would gain: peace in my busy home, and the ability my schedule gives me to accomplish the things I feel God wants me to do in my family." Tracy

"Making and using a schedule has helped me, and there were people who thought I was hopeless!" Sheri

Moms who have applied these methods have gained new hope from MOTH (*Managers of Their Homes*). They have moved from chaos, stress, and disorganization to peace, contentment, and productivity. You can as well!

For information visit: www.Titus2.com

Or call: (913) 772-0392

Managers of Their Chores

A Practical Guide to Children's Chores

By Steven and Teri Maxwell

In the same way that *Managers of Their Homes* helped tens of thousands of moms "get it all done," *Managers of Their Chores* helps families conquer the chore battle. The book and included ChorePack system have the potential to revolutionize the way your family accomplishes chores. Whether you are chore challenged or a seasoned chore warrior, you will gain motivation and loads of practical advice on implementing a stress-free chore system.

Many questions arise as families look at the issue of chores: Should children be expected to do chores? How many chores should they have? What age do we begin assigning chores? How do we encourage our children to accomplish their work? Is there a biblical basis for chores? Do chores bring benefits or burdens to our children? There are a multitude of questions that arise when we begin to discuss chores. *Managers of Their Chores* tackles these questions, giving answers and direction.

Written by parents of eight, *Managers of Their Chores* begins with the biblical foundation for chores and the many benefits chores will bring to a child—both now and in the future. It moves into key factors in parents' lives that will affect a chore system. The book gives pertinent information about what kinds of chores should reasonably be done in a home with children.

One chapter is devoted to helping moms work with their preschoolers on chores. For those moms who say they have no idea where to even begin, the book develops various pieces of a chore system and how it can be set up. Aspects of accountability, rewards, and consequences are addressed. Finally, *Managers of Their Chores* provides step-by-step directions for setting up a ChorePack chore system.

Managers of Their Chores comes with all the ChorePack materials typically needed for four children, including ChorePacks, chore card paper, and a ChorePack holder. In the appendix of the book, you will find a chore library with more than 180 chores listed, forms for use and future photocopying, and sample chore assignments from eight families.

Help prepare your children—from preschoolers to teens—for life by teaching them to do chores.

> *"I can't believe how much time we have gained in our days now that we have our ChorePack system in place." A mom*

> *"I have had chore lists for years, but this has been the best. It took prayer and time to get it set up, but we are reaping the benefits." A mom*

> *"It gave you visuals, explained the whys, needs, and benefits of chores, plus giving a system for implementing them. The book walked you through the process very clearly one step at a time with explanation of what to do and why." A mom*

For information visit: www.Titus2.com

Or call: (913) 772-0392

Keeping Our Children's Hearts

Our Vital Priority

By Steven and Teri Maxwell

Written for parents of young children to teenagers, this book shares the joys and outcomes of our vital priority—keeping our children's hearts. Rebellion and immorality are common among teens even within the Christian community. Does Scripture offer any path of hope for more than this for our children? What can parents do to direct their children toward godliness rather than worldliness? When does this process begin? What is the cost?

Steve and Teri Maxwell believe the key factors in raising children in the nurture and admonition of the Lord (Ephesians 6:4) are whether or not the parents have their children's hearts and what they are doing with those hearts. *Keeping Our Children's Hearts* offers direction and encouragement on this critically important topic.

Included in this book is a chapter co-authored by the three adult Maxwell children concerning their thoughts, feelings, experiences, and outcomes of growing up in a home where their parents wanted to keep their hearts.

> *"The most complete and most balanced book I have read on how to raise children who won't rebel!" Dr. S. M. Davis*

> *"This book is making me rethink what my purpose as a Christian, mother, and homeschooler should be." A mom*

To order or for more information: www.Titus2.com
Or call: (913) 772-0392

Preparing Sons
to Provide for a Single-Income Family
By Steven Maxwell

Steve Maxwell presents the groundwork for preparing your son to be a wage-earning adult. He gives practical suggestions and direction to parents for working with their sons from preschool age all the way through to adulthood. You will be challenged to evaluate your own life and the example you are setting for your son.

As the father of eight children, four of them now wage-earning adults, Steve has gained valuable experience he openly shares with other parents. Learn these principles from a dad whose twenty-four-year-old homeschooled son purchased a home debt free a year before his marriage, and whose second son has done the same. Steve explains how it is possible for parents, with a willing commitment, to properly prepare their sons to provide for a single-income family.

> *"You are dealing with topics that no one I know of has dealt with as thoroughly and practically as you have."* Dr. S. M. Davis

> "Preparing Sons *was a big blessing to my husband. All you ladies should get a copy for your husband and every church library needs one."* Shelly

Preparing Sons is available in paperback or unabridged audiobook.

To order or for more information: www.Titus2.com or www.PreparingSons.com
Or call: (913) 772-0392

Just Around the Corner
Encouragement and Challenge for
Christian Dads and Moms (Volumes 1 and 2)
By Steven and Teri Maxwell

Just Around the Corner (Volumes 1 and 2) is a compilation of Steve and Teri Maxwell's monthly Dad's and Mom's Corners. Steve's writing will challenge dads in their role as the spiritual head of the family. Teri's writing addresses many aspects of daily life that often frustrate or discourage a mom.

You will find the Mom's Corners grouped together in the front of the book and the Dad's Corners in the back. The Corners are all indexed so that you can read the ones relating to a specific topic you are interested in, if you so choose.

Topics addressed in *Just Around the Corner* include anger, child training, dads being the leaders of their families, depression, influencing children's spiritual outcome, homeschooling, husband/wife relationships, parenting, and much more!

With four of the Maxwell children now adults, Steve and Teri write from the perspective of having seen the truth of God's Word put into practice. At the same time, they are still in the trenches homeschooling four children.

"Just Around the Corner *has helped me to regain my focus and carry on to what God has called me to do.*" Michelle

"*It has been a HUGE blessing!!! It is a small dose of your larger message, very encouraging when I only need a pick-me-up or when I only have a few minutes.*" A mom

To order or for more information: www.Titus2.com

Or call: (913) 772-0392

The Moody Family Series
Summer with the Moodys
Autumn with the Moodys
Winter with the Moodys
Spring with the Moodys
By Sarah Maxwell

Often parents are concerned about negative examples and role models in books their children are reading. One goal in writing the Moody Family Series was to eliminate those kinds of examples replacing them with positive, godly ones.

In the four books, you'll find the Moodys helping a widowed neighbor, starting small businesses for the children, enjoying a family fun night, training their new puppy, homeschooling, Mom experiencing morning sickness, and much more! Woven throughout the books is the Moodys' love for the Lord and their enjoyment of time together. Children (parents too!) will enjoy Mr. and Mrs. Moody, Max, Mollie, Mitch, and Maddie—they'll come away challenged and encouraged.

"My six-year-old son asked Jesus into his heart while we were reading Autumn with the Moodys. *These books are wonderful, heart-warming Christian reading. The Moodys will always have a special place in our hearts!" A mom*

"At last, a Christian book series that is engaging and encourages my children to love Jesus more and bless their family and friends." A mom

To order or for more information: www.Titus2.com

Or call: (913) 772-0392

Audio Resources

Feed My Sheep:
A Practical Guide to Daily Family Devotions
By Steve Maxwell

Tried them and failed? Never tried because you knew it would be too big of a battle? No time for them even if you wanted to? Do any of these questions describe your experience with family devotions? This two CD set is highly motivational and practical.

In the first CD, Steve Maxwell gives realistic advice for achieving success with family devotions. He reveals the secret that he guarantees will work. The second CD contains two of the Maxwells' family devotions recorded live. You'll feel like you're right at home with Steve as you listen to him lead his family in their time in the Word. You will see how easy it is to lead your family in the most important time of the day.

Encouragement for the Homeschool Family

By the Maxwells

Encouragement for the Homeschool Family is an eight-session audio seminar which will encourage, exhort, and equip homeschooling families.

To order or for more information, www.Titus2.com.

Websites
www.Titus2.com
www.ChorePacks.com
www.FamiliesforJesus.com
www.HomeschooleCards.com
www.PreparingSons.com
www.PreparingDaughters.com